Diary Of An Ordinary Housewife

Diary Of An Ordinary Housewife

From The Ordinary,
Through The Extraordinary,
To The Piece Within

Maile Page

White Falcon
Publishing
www.whitefalconpublishing.com

Diary Of An Ordinary Housewife
Maile Page

www.whitefalconpublishing.com

Requests for permission should be addressed to
mailepage11@gmail.com

ISBN - 978-1-63640-438-7

To Tei and Haley,
my ordinary, extraordinary children.

Table of Contents

PART I: THE ORDINARY

PART III: THE PIECE WITHIN

Acknowledgments

They say it takes a village to raise a child. For me, this book was that "child" trying to be born for many years. I want to thank the "village", whose love, guidance, and support helped this book to be conceived, grow, and finally come forth into the world.

To my editor and good friend Mari Florence, this book would not exist without your brilliance, insights, and loving support. You are simply amazing. Thank you for taking this intense journey with me.

To Howard Cohl of Cohl Media, who believed in this project early on, connected me with the right people at the right time, and helped me stay the course.

To all my teachers, who introduced me to the miracle of energy and energy healing. To Christina Thomas Fraser for gifting me with my first physical experience of my energy body and training me to help others release trapped emotional trauma. Meeting you, I believe, saved my life, if I may be so dramatic. To Sondra and Markus Ray, for your amazing ability to identify and heal negative birth patterns and for helping me take that leap of faith toward freedom that allowed me to grow and pursue higher dreams. To my Quantum Energetics Structured Therapy teachers, Raedene and Steve VandenHeuvel, Bernie and Kathy Finch, and Judith Heath, for dedicating your lives to making available an energy-strengthening modality that is unparalleled in the world. Your collective humility and astounding understanding of human body functioning are miraculous. To Dr. Les Feinberg, for your many years dedicated to developing the NeuroModulation Technique. Your brilliant mind is surpassed only by your unique approach to healing. I am positive that modality saved my mother's life and the life of a dear friend—twice.

A big thank you to my special friends. To Elizabeth Terrel, who introduced me to Quantum Energetics Structured Therapy and without whom I may still be trying to find my "passion." Your friendship has been a blessing, a great comfort, and an inspiration. Richard Skeie, who taught me so much about awakening, the mind-body connection, and the many voices within my head. Kevin Kidd, who is the best basket holder this side of Kansas, and whose wisdom and loving support helped birth this book many times when it was stuck in the birth canal. You are an amazing healer and Galactic Ambassador. Archna Mehta, my partner in crime, with whom I have shared many amazing metaphysical adventures. Thank you for your friendship, your wisdom, and your heart. I am so grateful to have met you. Thank you, Sanjeev Anand, whose Divine guidance and powerful Yagyas and Poojas helped this book to be created with the right timing and with great blessings. Soko Ushijima, my "sister" and best friend. The eleven-year-old me is so lucky to have met the eleven-year-old you. There is no one like you in the world. Thank you for you.

To my parents, who I know are in my soul family, and honored their spiritual agreement to join me in this life and provide amazing opportunities for learning, growth, and expansion. You did your job well. Thank you.

To my son Tei. As a child, you delighted, and as an adult, you inspire me with your determination, courage, wisdom, insights, heart, and love. We continue to support each other, experiencing the same journey on different paths. It has been and continues to be a blessing and an honor to know you. To my daughter Haley and fellow INFJ. In this "House of Illusions", you and I have ridden the tallest waves together and survived them all. Your honesty, integrity, humor, beauty (inner and outer), talents, and heart has been and continue to be a blessing.

Introduction

I am aware how risky it is to start my introduction with the sentence below. But that sentence is in keeping with my edict for this book: No Fear. So, here goes.

In 2006, I received a five-hour astrological reading. In it, the reader mentioned that in 2015 I would publish one of two books I was "supposed" to write. Perhaps, because the reading was so darn long and specific and because many of the things she mentioned were accurate, I took those words to heart. But instead of being inspiring, they became a burden.

For years I kept asking intuitives and channelers, "Do you see a book in my energy? Does it tell you what I am supposed to write?" I also tried writing several books, trying to get a heads up on those two books.

When struggling with parenting, armed only with the tool of timeouts instead of the yelling, threats, and spankings of my day, I thought perhaps I was supposed to write a book on parenting. Many of my friends said the creative parenting tools I had discovered would make a great book. But, I was too busy *doing* said parenting and had no time for writing.

Year after year, no matter what my life circumstances, I felt the burden of that book directive from long ago simmering in the back of my mind. Then life got complicated. I was facing my impending divorce and all the emotional turmoil that entailed. I was a single mother trying to find my way. Then I started my own healing center and all the learning curves that presented.

I was also parenting older children whose problems were much more complicated and heart-wrenching than making sure they had clean diapers, food, and rest. I forgot about the books. I was too busy living my life. Then one day, while I was at the airport, on my way to visit my son at the University of Tennessee, I spotted a book in the airport snack shop.

It was titled *The One Thing.*[1] The book suggested that shotgunning our efforts, instead of focusing on the one thing that was most important, was the reason we weren't attaining our long-held goals. For some reason, this book really spoke to me. Looking at my life at that time, I was definitely all over the place.

I was running The Centre and organizing many classes and events. I was trying to learn the technology to create online classes. I was constantly on the lookout for the next healing modality I needed to learn and much more. It dawned on me, I was treading water, just like the book described, and getting nowhere.

When I asked myself, as the book suggested, what was the one thing I really wanted to accomplish. I realized it was that book I was told I would write all those years ago. The pull to write it was strong now, and I was ready. I realized that all that I had experienced during my transition from law to energy healing was what I wanted to write. I also realized it was 2015.

The book you are holding was the book I wanted to write. The editor I was paired with, someone who had worked in six of the major publishing houses and who I trusted and respected, said, "No one wants to read your memoir. You are not famous. You need to write a book that helps people learn to do energy healing themselves."

I thought a book that simplified the energy healing process would be so contracted it would be useless, and I told her as much. With much convincing, she said it was possible to write a book that was both simple and helpful to the masses. She said my background in litigation where, in court, I had eight seconds to grab a judge's attention by distilling complex legal theories into easily understood reasons why my client should win would help me write this unusual book.

After much hair-pulling, headaches, and declarations that, "I cannot do this" and "I quit", *The Infinite Now* was published in February 2020. The timing of that publication went just like you might imagine a publication would go in the middle of a world pandemic—not good.

Throughout the writing of that first book, I was told many times, "No, you can't put that in there. No one would believe that. No, change 'grapefruit-sized cyst' to just 'cyst'. No one would believe that three grapefruit-sized cysts dissolved under your fingertips. You will come across as nuts," etc.

I vowed that the next book I write, the one I wanted to write all along, would include all the parts of my story deemed too wacky for prime time. If I was thought of as nutty at best and an outright liar at worst, so be it.

I figured since the first book was completed, I could take a break and contemplate the second book. Not so. I received a call in late September 2021 from Archna, my Vedic astrologer friend, saying she received a call from India. Her good friend, an amazing Vedic astrologer, Sanjeev Anand,[2] and the one who oversaw and conducted our monthly poojas[3] called her.

He said, "Call Maile and urge her to write that book by October 19th." Archna explained, "Despite Mercury being in retrograde, the cosmic energies support getting the book done fast."

"Fast? Are you insane?" I asked Archna. That gives me a month to write, edit, and proofread the whole manuscript. She insisted I would have assistance (on the other side), and I could do it. I have to admit this strained our friendship for a few days, as I questioned her sanity and the quality of this "ill-advised" advice.

I texted my good friend and trusted editor, Mari Florence. I told her of the proposed book deadline I received. From working with me for several years, she was no longer surprised by strange comments like, "the cosmic energies support getting the book done by October 19th."

I asked her, "Is this insane? Do you think this is possible?" "I'm in if you're in," was her response. It didn't flow without obstacles. Mari and I supported each other through several wall-hitting episodes. But, we listened to our bodies when uninspired and followed the thread of creativity when visible.

You may notice the book does not flow in a linear fashion. As far as facts go, I jump around at times referencing events that happened in the past, then refer to future events, only to circle back to events I have already mentioned. This is because the realizations that came from this experience did not occur in a one-direction trajectory. Rather, they emerged after much contemplation. They encompassed reflections on the past, comparing thoughts from my younger and older self, and realizations that could only come from hindsight. This made the writing of this book tricky at times. For those of you who have read *The Infinite Now,* you may have noticed that some of the examples and anecdotes have been repurposed for this book. Miraculous events are not an everyday occurrence, so I've reused some stories to illustrate my points better.

I have no doubt that Archna was right about there being assistance on the other side. There will be someone out there, I suspect, who will comment, "Yeah, you get what you pay for. Her speed writing is a pile o'crap." I don't fault or condemn those who think that. I would probably have that thought as well.

What I do know is that this book comes from a place of wanting to help fellow beings who might be running as fast as they can on their own personal hamster wheels, feeling like they are getting nowhere. This book is for those that also feel that "void" within that cannot seem to be filled with the finite treasures of the world (happiness, health, wealth, success, status, reputation, etc.).

This is not a book telling you how to be the best you can be. This book invites you to consider that you may be looking at the wrong "you" and that the "you" you aren't seeing is perfect as is, no matter what is occurring in your life. Don't blindly believe me. Read on, and discover for yourself if what I share holds true for you—the TRUE You.

Part I

The Ordinary

Chapter 1

Present Day

Each time my mom's senior living facility calls, my heart skips a beat. Lately, she's been falling a lot. There have been a few trips to the emergency room, but surprisingly (or not), she has a pretty thick skull. Yet, today is different. She had fallen asleep in her chair and broken her fall with her face. Bleeding profusely, she is hysterical, worried that she has knocked out her two front teeth.

When I got to the hospital, the nurses told me that they had to medicate her to calm her down and treat her. My mother does not tolerate any form of pain well, and the lack of control even less. So much so that she apparently ripped out her IV line and swung her fist at the nurse trying to restrain her.

It turns out we got lucky: she did not knock out her front teeth. The doctors ruled out a concussion but suggested we go to her regular dentist to get a thorough exam. My mom is sheepish when she climbs into the passenger seat, confessing, "I don't think I was a very good patient." I found that to be an ironic confession for a woman who worked as a nurse for 35 years.

I feel sad that she is incoherent most days now. Even last year, at 82 years old, she would vacillate between lucid conversation and nonsense, recalling bits and pieces of the past. But lately, there are long stretches of incoherent babbling. It often feels as if she has already died, and I am mourning her loss, even as she sits next to me in the car.

The ER staff assures me she is sore but OK, so I take her back to her facility. About four days later, as we are driving to the dentist, she says her teeth feel weird and that she can't eat properly. Remember when I said that my mom babbles incoherently much of the time? Yet not so when it comes to practical things like her exercise regimen (doing laps with her walker within her senior home), observing the people around her, and food (eating was always a top contender in her list of favorite activities).

I have parked the car now, and I turn toward her. "Look at me and show me your teeth," I ask. She presents her teeth with a wide fake smile. Sure enough, her bite looks out of alignment. Instead of her front teeth resting in front of her lower teeth, they are landing smack on top of her lower teeth, creating a gap between her upper and lower set of teeth. She says, "See, I cannot close my jaw properly, and I cannot chew right."

Once upstairs in the office, the dentist shows me her x-ray, pointing out a white line that traverses her mandible, the bone in her jaw that holds her upper teeth. He explains that this line indicates a fracture from her fall and that her upper teeth were displaced, creating a gap in the back of her bite. This is what is making it difficult to eat. The dentist says that the gap is caused by her front teeth resting on top of her lower teeth rather than in front as they should be.

He then advises that I take her to an oral surgeon for a consultation and warns that if her mandible heals in this misaligned position, she will have ongoing problems that will require surgery. When I ask him what the oral surgeon can do for her, he replies that he's not sure what *anyone* can do for her. Ominous.

Once we're back in the car, I get on the phone with the oral surgeon's office to make the appointment. The secretary explains that my mom's consultation is not covered by her dental insurance because this is not a dental issue and was technically an accident. She further explains that when we arrive, they will take x-rays and proceed from there.

I really don't feel like taking her for x-rays that have already been taken and will tell them what we already know. I then look at my mom with some sadness. Eating is one of the few pleasures she really enjoys these days. Jaw surgery is very painful, not to mention seriously expensive.

What I did next requires a bit of explaining and some backstory (which will come later). This detail will either pique your interest or cause you to hurl this book across the room into the trash. Don't worry about it: I am not attached to your reaction either way. I have had both reactions many times over the years and have learned reactions are not about me—so I don't take them too personally. I hope this detail doesn't offend, and you keep reading.

After working for ten years as a litigator, my life took a 20-year detour into the world of energy medicine.

How and why this happened is a long story that I'll reveal in upcoming chapters. Suffice it to say, two decades of energy medicine offers options not available in ordinary circumstances. But, even after practicing for all these years, there was still so much I didn't know. This situation with my mom was no different, and I was at a loss of how to proceed.

I text my teacher[4], explaining the situation with my mother, and ask her what she thinks I should do. She suggests performing the extrusion and sutural separation codes to move the upper teeth back in alignment. She warns me not to do the fracture code until I have the dentist confirm her teeth are back in alignment, or her teeth will heal out of alignment.

I look up the codes on my phone, quickly do them, then I just sit there wondering what to do now. The codes were simple and painless to perform, and my mom hardly knew I'd done anything. (Codes are energy corrections used in the energy healing work in which I was trained. Each energy correction lends extra energy to the body, much like one provides air during CPR to one who cannot breathe. The codes correspond to numerical frequencies that remove energetic blocks in the body, restoring its innate ability to heal.)

I am staring blankly out the window when my mom says, "Hey, my teeth feel better." I turn to look at her, and, sure enough, her upper teeth are now resting in front of her lower teeth. She is able to close her jaw properly now. I really think I am hallucinating. I quickly call the dentist's office and ask them if I can bring my mom back up for a quick recheck.

The secretary says to come back in an hour. By now, my mom hasn't eaten in four hours. She is a tiny woman with virtually no body fat. Hence, she gets hangry something fierce when she doesn't eat. So I dash across the street to Starbucks and get her a blueberry scone. To my surprise, she immediately and delightedly chomps away, exclaiming, "I can eat now. I haven't been able to eat right since I fell!"

Back in the dentist's office, he reexamines her bite and says slowly, "Her bite definitely looks like it moved." He shows me how there is no gap now between her upper and lower teeth in the back of her bite. He then looks at me but has no explanation.

I take a breath and explain that I do this type of energy healing, but that I don't tell many people because they generally don't understand. I also told him that I didn't want to do the fracture code until I made sure her teeth were back in alignment. Then I ask him sheepishly if he would be willing to redo her x-ray before I take her to the oral surgeon. To my complete surprise, he agrees and tells me to bring her in the next morning. It was very surprising since many doctors would simply say it would be a waste of time, and the result wouldn't be any different.

So I do the fracture code on my mom. As I drive her home, she is pointing to me smiling, saying, "I know you did this. You did that thing that you do, didn't you? I knew you could help me." I was as surprised by her vote of confidence as I was by her quick recovery. Even though I do this for a living, I was still astonished by the outcome. *One thing I have noticed, in my practice, is I get my very best results with loved ones.*

The next morning, we're back at the dentist's office. The dental assistant is questioning why we are redoing my mom's x-ray since it was just taken the day before. She posts the film, and I look at it. I cannot see the white line from the previous afternoon's x-ray, which indicated there was a hairline fracture. When the dentist comes in, I watch his back as he reviews the new x-ray. He stares at it and doesn't say a thing. He then clicks on the image from the previous day. He clicks back and forth between the x-rays, saying nothing.

After what seems like a long time, he turns to me and says slowly, "The fracture isn't as visible in this second x-ray." He seems hesitant now as he looks at me. He shows me her front teeth are not perfectly back in alignment but are pretty darn close. He says when she bites down, her lower teeth push out her front teeth a bit. I am OK with that, and I assure him that I will still take my mom to see the oral surgeon. He nods, approving of that game plan.

As I leave, and I don't know if I am being paranoid, the usually über-friendly staff stare at me warily as I leave, as if, in the privacy of my home, I wear a tinfoil hat and communicate regularly with aliens. I am used to this by now, but I still feel bummed because our easygoing, friendly exchange is now gone.

When I take my mom to the oral surgeon a few days later, the doctor looks at her teeth and x-rays and confirms there is no fracture, and her teeth are in alignment. He has that friendly demeanor of a doctor who enjoys delivering good news.

He compared his new x-ray with the x-ray sent from the dentist's office (that showed the fracture) and said he wasn't sure why it was no longer fractured, but sometimes fractures heal over time. He doesn't notice it has only been a few days since the first x-ray was taken. I say nothing about my intervention and shrug with him agreeing, "Yeah, who knows," and "Yay, what good luck for us." I don't want to take the chance that this office also puts me in "loon" status. He is relaxed and feeling gracious delivering this good news and says the visit is gratis.

I think it is interesting that even though many in the general population have heard that energy exists all around and within us, many still do not know or realize that that very energy has the capability of effecting physical change when the energetic intention is strong enough. Until I experienced this myself and with my clients, I too did not realize the extensive physical capabilities of directed energy.

I was grateful for this turn of events. It doesn't always happen this way, but the fact that it did sometimes seemed like a wacky, miraculous blessing. What seems unfathomable to most is normal life for us. It reflects a reality that seems to defy the constraints of life in the third dimension, not in a loud dramatic way, but in a quiet, matter-of-fact way.

When I first began writing this book, my former editor told me that no one wants to hear my story because I am not a celebrity. Yet, in defiance of her expert opinion, I will tell it anyway. If you read my experiences and believe them, your reality can't help but also be transformed. When your mind expands, your life expands. Who doesn't want that?

Chapter 2

Monday Is A Good Day To Die
(The Ordinary Journey Begins)

According to statistics from the U.S. Centers for Disease Control (CDC), suicides occur more frequently on Monday than any other day of the week.[5] It makes sense. Most people I know hate their jobs, so the beginning of a dreaded work week seems like the best day to exit.

After working in litigation for ten years, I could confidently state that I hated practicing law. Everyone thinks that law is an enviable career; one of status and big bucks. I certainly did when I chose my career. Yet, the reality is you have to account for every six minutes of your day and report a minimum of six-to-eight billable hours for the firm Every Single Day. This means that going to the bathroom, chatting at the water cooler, and eating lunch are luxuries, and you will end up working anywhere from ten to fourteen hours a day to meet that daily billing requirement.

Regardless of billable hours, the work is endless, and your salary is capped. So, by the time you factor in the actual hours you spend working, you are paid no better than the person serving you Big Macs® at McDonald's. It's true: I actually did the math one day, deciding to waste a precious six minutes to indulge myself in an emotional rant.

The most distasteful part of the job is with whom you spend the majority of your day. They are people called "hired guns" and are retained to fight for a living. So this means that those long hours of six-minute accountability are spent with people who spend their entire working lives arguing. Can you see how McDonald's seemingly fares better?

I used to fantasize about dying. Not killing myself, but just not being alive anymore. I was miserable. I don't know why I didn't just quit. I think that, like most attorneys, after spending all that time and energy on an expensive higher education, it's hard to walk away from your investment.

It wasn't until I had my first child, my son, that I started to rebel. There was this one partner at the firm, a woman who never had children and who seemed hell-bent to prove women could *not* have both a career and children. Behind her back, one attorney told me she was called the "relationship destroyer" because she made sure weekends and holidays were just words and not a reality.

It didn't surprise me then that, shortly after returning from maternity leave, I was reassigned to work with this partner. I, along with three or four attorneys, would sit in her office while she made the air unbreathable with her chain-smoking (this was before smoking indoors was banned). We watched the top of her head (not a billable event) while she made phone calls, dictated letters, and barked orders to her secretary. We were tasked to research and write legal briefs but were not allowed to leave her office to research and write said briefs.

This torment could go on until 8 or 9 p.m. It felt like a law jail. If I were actually working, it would be different, but I resented not being home with my son so I could sit there imprisoned. One day I was just fed up. It was 8 p.m., and I sat there, daring myself to do the unthinkable. Silently counting to three, I suddenly stood up and announced, "I'll be right back" (presumably to get something from my office or go to the restroom). Instead, I walked to my office, grabbed my things, and walked out the door. I was told after half an hour she asked the other attorneys, "Do you think she left?" I guess not playing the game was the little-known escape clause from this legal torture because shortly thereafter, I was reassigned to another partner.

Life at the law firm wasn't all bad. There was one person at the firm that made life bearable, inspirational even. I don't know how we became friends, but there was this word processor (typists assigned to type long legal documents) that I'll call Michelle. She became like a spiritual teacher to me. She taught me about meditation, about our energy fields, about people who could communicate with animals, about intuition, and even enlightenment. I knew nothing about this metaphysical world and had tremendous respect for her. My misery at the firm had opened my mind and heart to what she had to share.

Across from my desk, there were two chairs for clients. Behind the chairs was a blank white wall. One day I began to see what can only be described as a cloud of color that glowed around clients' heads and shoulders as they sat across from me. When I mentioned this to Michelle, she explained this was the aura, an energy field that expands around people's bodies, that was especially strong about the head and shoulders.

Michelle said you could tell a lot about a person by the color of that energy field around them. Black or brown could be fatigue or depression, and red streaks indicated rage or anger. Blue indicated spirituality and love of family. Green indicated health or impending wealth. Yellow was strong when people were thinking. People who felt self-conscious, scared, or were lying had energy fields that contracted close to their bodies in a narrow band.

I recall one day when I was taking a deposition (when you question a witness or party under oath, and the typed transcript is later used as evidence at trial). This plaintiff (the party suing for damages) was crucial in establishing liability. During most of her testimony, I noticed her energy field extended six-to-eight inches around her head and shoulders. When I came to the questions that had a direct effect on her case, I closely observed her energy field just out of curiosity.

I could barely sit still when, in response to a key question, her energy field went from a yellow fluffy cloud to a narrow brownish band that quickly contracted around her head and shoulders. I took note, and when I received the transcript, I wrote "lying" in the margin as a reminder.

When my supervising partner was reviewing the case to evaluate whether we should settle or take the case to court, he came across my note and queried me. "Why did you write 'lying' in the margin here? This is a pretty crucial question." I didn't want to seem nutty, so I said, "I don't know, I just had the feeling she was lying," He replied, "You do realize we can't rely on your hunch as evidence at trial?" He walked away, shaking his head. This was one of many head-shaking incidents that would come in the months ahead.

Another time, a partner came into my office and overheard the tail end of a conversation I was having with Michelle about an animal communicator who solved the mystery of the belligerent zoo elephant. This elephant, normally docile and easygoing, had become aggressive, even toward the zookeeper whom she loved. After consulting with many veterinarians, the zookeeper was getting desperate. His wife told him about this woman who communicates with animals, and because he was out of options, he hired her.

This animal communicator was given no information, other than this elephant had become aggressive, and they didn't know what caused this sudden change or how to help her. During the next several hours of sessions, the elephant "told" her she had just given birth. Right after the birth, they took her baby with no explanation. The animal communicator relayed this information to the zookeeper, who confirmed that she did give birth, but the baby elephant was stillborn, and they took the baby away so as not to upset the mother.

The zookeeper got the skull of the baby elephant, which they had kept, and brought it to the mother, who instinctively knew it was her baby's skull. She immediately grabbed the skull and rolled it around as she let out loud trumpets of pain and grief. Given the opportunity to know what happened and to grieve properly, this mother received the closure she needed and soon returned to her normal agreeable temperament.

I was amazed by this story. For me, it opened a whole new world that included animals communicating mentally with pictures. Michelle explained that animals do not communicate with words like humans. They read and send messages via mental images. This is why when your dog pees on the carpet, and you yell, "No!" while picturing him peeing on the carpet, the dog "hears" pee on the carpet. I would experience this myself in future months.

This conversation did not sit well with the partner who overheard it. Shortly thereafter, the firm circulated a memo strongly suggesting that, in the interest of having an efficient work environment, personal relationships between attorneys and support staff were discouraged.

This friendship would also end my current life path, my marriage, and any semblance of life as I knew it then. This is not to say it was her fault. It certainly was not. But, after she introduced concepts and experiences so removed from my current reality, my life could not stay the same. The resulting gulf between my husband and I would prove too enormous for us to continue relating in any workable fashion. But that will all unfold in the coming pages.

Chapter 3

Heads I Win, Tails You Raise The Kids

After our daughter was born, my husband and I started arguing over who would quit and raise the kids. Taking a hiatus from the law is career suicide in a profession where the first ten years of your career are spent vying for that coveted partnership position. And, unlike other careers, more years of experience can work against you. In fact, unless you have extensive or specialized experience, it makes no sense to change firms. The new firm can't mold you to work as they want, and that is very important to law firms.

My husband saw the situation similarly. Having my son slowed me down a lot, work-wise, so I had probably blown any chance for partnership already. At least this was his argument for me to take a hiatus from work. We probably sound like terrible parents, but in those early years, our work success was our identity.

I couldn't really argue with his logic. My husband was right: I was the most logical choice for becoming the stay-at-home parent, at least until the children reached kindergarten. And, in keeping with my driven personality, I simply refocused all my energy and ambition toward my new role.

One issue that immediately arose was the uncontrollable nature of toddlers. I naively believed that, with enough time and research, I was going to solve the mystery of parenting strong-willed and tantrum-prone toddlers. Since this was my new career, I decided to dedicate all my energy to this endeavor. I spent months trying to find the formula for getting control of my House of Toddlers. Spoiler alert: You can't control toddlers. At best, you can offer choices and create distractions, but direct control is not possible without resorting to old-school parenting (threats and spankings), which I was *not* about to do.

If it isn't obvious yet, I have *teeny-weeny* control issues. And by teeny weeny, I mean Huge. And speaking of control issues, I wasn't used to being out of the loop in our household management, and I certainly wasn't used to not having control over my financial security.

I started hovering over my husband's law practice. I'm sure I was making him crazy. I hounded him with questions about his cases, making sure he was staying on top of things. He had this one appellate argument (the place you go for a second opinion when the court rules against your client) that I was fixated on. There were boxes and boxes of documents to review and an appellate brief to write.

My husband was a consummate procrastinator and wasn't working on his argument for the appellate hearing. This was majorly stressing me out; given my control issues, his procrastination equated to failure and financial ruin. This was a big deal, and he seemed unfazed about the fast-approaching hearing date. One night, I uncharacteristically prayed for help for my husband. I wasn't expecting the form of help when it arrived.

My husband was sleeping in the spare bedroom to escape my postpartum snoring when I woke up, wide awake, at 4 a.m. with the organization for the entire appellate argument floating in my head. I grabbed some paper and quickly started writing as fast as I could. The outline was very simple. It listed each legal issue, with his best argument and supporting evidence and the opposing argument and their supporting evidence. The outline covered every legal issue in the case in this format. When I was done writing two hours later, the outline was 16 pages long.

I was shocked when I started reading what I had written. I had no idea from where it came. Yes, I had asked about the case, but I had not read the boxes of documents and was not that knowledgeable about the case. Just as I finished, my husband had awakened and walked past me to the bathroom to get ready for work. He asked, "What are you writing?" I held out the pages to him, "I did an outline for your appellate argument." He laughed, "OK," rolling his eyes mockingly. Feeling defensive, I said, "Fine, give it back." He was reading the first page and slowly mumbled, "No, I'll take a look at this later at work."

He said nothing about it later that day or that week, and I soon forgot I had written it. Somehow the writing of it had eased my anxiety. On the day of the appellate hearing, he returned home very happy and excited.

The partners from New York had flown in for the hearing to watch him argue the case. The hearing was a huge success, and he was flying high. I said, "I guess you never read that outline?" He said, "I never told you?" I said, "Tell me what?"

Then he said, after he got to work, he read the outline and had his secretary type it up. He had used it to help prepare for the hearing. He said, "When I got to the hearing, the judge went down that outline like it was a script he and I were performing." He said he couldn't believe it. His court performance appeared very prepared and impressive, and the outcome of the hearing was favorable.

I knew in my heart that I was not the author of that outline, and I wondered how that information came through. I would learn in years to come that it was a form of channeling (when information comes through a person when they get out of the way, so to speak). I'll share more about this later.

Despite that breakthrough, I had many other challenges. It turns out that my lack of control over our finances was the least of my worries. When you aren't distracted by 16-hour workdays, past emotional trauma can come floating to the surface and bite you in the butt.

But, in the meantime, there were perks to this new assignment, like trips to the zoo and the park. Hanging out with toddlers is also fun. Everything is new to them, and being a first-hand witness to their delight and fascination about the world is a true blessing.

Chapter 4

Auras, And Lions, And Bears, Oh My!

I have a confession. When I began seeing auras around people's heads and shoulders at work, it made me feel special. I liked that. Amidst the piles of paper and stress, there was another reality that was hidden from view; a technicolor show swirling around everyone, broadcasting their thoughts, emotions, and spiritual inner workings.

I wanted to expand and perfect this ability. I started reading every book on auras and intuition I could find. Truth be told, I wanted to see images of the future. I would discover years later that what was really fueling all my metaphysical ambition was a need for control. (There it is again. Do you sense a theme here?) I wanted information that could safeguard my health, wealth, and happiness.

Little did I know that this need for control was blocking my intuitive development. It turns out that intuition is a subtle energy that hides when the mind hijacks the process. Developing intuition and the ability to see subtle energies, like auras, is less about ability and more about relaxing and noticing that which is always present but largely ignored. It's a fleeting ability that floats in and out of its own accord that I find frustrating even to this day.

Surprisingly, my intuition developed on its own when I spent time with my two toddlers. The difference between work and life with small children is you must be fully present at all times with toddlers. They are on the move every second, and even brushing your teeth or going to the bathroom is a risk, lest you return to find these beings dancing on the kitchen table or dangling from the support rod of the garage door (both real events in my household). I did not appreciate the gift of being fully present until I noticed those intuitive abilities I had been unsuccessfully hunting down at work were drifting in on their own while hanging out with these two sentient beings.

Two outings with them stand out.

My kids loved the zoo. During one visit, I remember we were in front of the elephant exhibit when I suddenly felt nauseous and could not see out of my left eye. Startled, I thought I might be having a stroke. Next to us was a woman who was asking the zookeeper, "How old is she? How is she doing?" The zookeeper replied that the elephant was getting on in years, and she was not well and was blind in her left eye.

What? Was it possible I was picking up the energy of this elephant? I quickly pushed the stroller away from the elephant exhibit and noticed as I got further away, nausea started to lift, and sight returned in my left eye. I was trying to understand how this could happen. Were we all connected? Are diseases contagious on an energetic level?

When we arrived at the tigers' exhibit, I reached down to retrieve juice boxes and Goldfish® crackers from the stroller. While hunched over, I had a sudden feeling of overwhelming grief. It felt unbearable. I looked into the exhibit and noticed there was only one tiger when there had always been two. I realized that the grief I was feeling was the tiger's. I noticed a zoo worker approaching in a golf cart and flagged him down. I asked, "Where is the other tiger?" He replied, "Yeah, it's sad. The other tiger died yesterday."

To my horror, I started sobbing, not crying, sobbing, and said, "He is so sad. You have to get him another tiger to keep him company." His chuckle was mortifying. It highlighted the over-the-top nature of my behavior. He patted my arm and said, "I know, we are working on it. Just try to enjoy the day, honey." I felt embarrassed at my outburst and also self-conscious that he might think I was a nut. I meekly nodded in agreement. My children were now looking on with concern. Why was Mommy sobbing at the zoo? Embarrassment notwithstanding, I felt excited that I was picking up energies around me without even trying. My response was to read more books and try to harness and develop these abilities.

The second incident happened at the beach. We live an hour from the beach, so I had not ventured this far with them before. I wanted my children to smell the fresh sea breeze, hear the seagulls, and build sandcastles, so one day, I took them there.

On this day, the beach was deserted. We were completely alone. The sky was overcast, but the weather was perfect. As I watched my children kneeling in the sand digging a large hole, I suddenly noticed huge colored clouds of energy around their heads and bodies. I had never seen such large and colorful energies before or since. The energies expanded at least three feet around them and were bright orange, green, yellow, and magenta.

I sat mesmerized by the dancing colors swirling around them. Hours went by as they played, and I watched. Even now, I can picture those colors and that day on the beach. I laughed when my son said the next day, "Let's go to the beach again. We can play while you look at us."

I realized one of the reasons I could see their auras better was the expanse of sand. The white sand created a blank canvas against which the subtle colors could be seen. When there are other objects in the room, they create a colored backdrop which makes it harder to see this subtle energy. Second, the children felt happy and relaxed. This allowed their auras to expand much wider than I had witnessed around people stressed in the work environment.

I then asked the kids to stand in front of a white wall at home as I practiced trying to see their auras. They quickly grew impatient. Being stared at while playing at the beach was one thing. This was boring and weird.

I then discovered that if I stood in the bathroom and looked in the mirror, the closed bathroom door created a white background behind me. Now, I could see the space around my head and shoulders against a white background. This is how I practiced seeing my own aura. I realized if I softened my gaze and did not look directly at my head, I could see the aura better.

It was during this time that I read a story about Edgar Cayce, a famous intuitive who would go into a trance, retrieve valuable healing information, and then relay it to his clients. On one occasion, he was in a department store and was about to enter an elevator. He was so startled at the appearance of the people in the elevator, he stepped back and did not enter. After the elevator door closed, the elevator cable snapped, and the people in the elevator plunged to their deaths.

Edgar realized what was so unusual about the people in the elevator. He could not see their auras. He was so used to seeing auras that people looked odd without them. He concluded their impending death was the reason they had no auras.

After learning this story, I made it a practice to check for peoples' auras just after boarding airplanes. I still don't know what I will do if someday, while on a plane, I cannot see everyone's auras. I can imagine doing nothing, then plunging to my death in the eventual plane crash, rather than embarrassing myself by asking to disembark the plane with no rational explanation.

The discovery that people and animals have energy fields that expand from their bodies was a first step in learning more about energy. I soon learned that energy could, with intent, be directed toward and felt by others.

Chapter 5

Gift Love, Take Love

In my defense, I think everyone smothers their loved ones, especially their pets, with hugs and kisses. This looks like gratuitous affection, but in reality, we are often seeking, not offering, love and comfort.

When my children were younger, I would often reach out to hug and kiss them, murmuring that I loved them. In response, I would get a foot to the chest or a hand pushing my face away. Or they might turn away and say, "Stop smothering me!"

I never thought much of it. I would laugh and think it was part of our affectionate ritual. I rationalized that the children didn't appreciate the constant stream of affection. They take it for granted, I would say to myself.

Then, I was reading an Osho[6] book in which he described the difference between "Gift vs. Take Love." He said love was an energy that was either flowing to or from us. He explained that what most people thought of as love was really an expectation for the other person to make us feel a certain way; loved, safe, respected, adored, etc. When people feel less than whole, they seek wholeness through union with another, he said.

"Gift love," he explained, is when two people feel whole and share that wholeness. They don't need the other person as much as they are sharing their mutual wholeness as a spiritual dance. I have read that relationships are personal growth assignments. The purpose is to heal past emotional traumas in this and past lives. When spiritual growth is gained or a lesson is learned, the relationship will begin to feel flat and fall away naturally. This creates room for a new relationship, with new growth and healing opportunities.

We don't stress when a tree in our yard loses all its leaves in winter because we know this is a natural process, and new leaves and fruit will blossom in the spring. Yet, often we cannot have the same insight and acceptance when relationships organically end.

Osho believed 99 percent of relationships were based on "take love" rather than gift love because everyone wanted something from the other person they didn't have within themselves already, like self-respect, self-love, self-assuredness. He said we are most attracted to those that have something we think we are lacking.

I thought about this and reevaluated my interactions with my children. I had to admit that perhaps my intentions were seeking rather than giving affectionate energy. If I were being honest, many times, my overtures of affection were really a need for comfort, affection, or reassurance they loved me.

One morning, I spotted Haley (then six years old) walking down the hallway. It was a school day, and we were getting ready to leave. I thought I would test Osho's theory. I knelt down and wrapped my arms around her tiny body and imagined love energy emitting from my heart and encircling her. This time she didn't push me away. She stood still with her eyes closed and murmured, "Oh, Mommy, you just sent me to heaven." I was the one who finally ended the embrace. She remained standing, eyes closed, with a contented smile on her face.

All of a sudden, I had a realization: It wasn't what we did in life, but the intention with which we did it. Our energy is not static. It is a vibrating field awaiting our instructions (our intent). So a simple hug could be giving or taking energy, depending on our intent. That is why charity offered with compassion and humility feels different than charity given with an air of superiority and pity. Amazing.

Then I considered all of my relationships with work colleagues, friends, and family. I thought of how every time my mother visited, even for a few days, I would feel exhaustion that would take days to shift. My mom would follow me everywhere. I couldn't even go to the bathroom without her following me. I would literally have to say, "Um, I got this." She would realize where she had followed me, laugh, and then sit on my bed, waiting for me.

I knew my mom had a shaky relationship with her mom. Grandma was pretty critical. I think my mom thought she created this being (me) whose sole purpose was to make her feel loved. It was a burdensome life task that I feel to this day.

After learning the difference between gift vs. take love, I was better able to set boundaries. There was no judgment, just discernment. I consciously retained my energy and did not allow it to be drained by people seeking wholeness they can generate from within.

Learning how we can direct our energy fields with intention was fascinating, but I still wanted to understand how this energy fits within the framework of our lives. I would soon receive a message that would take me years to understand.

Chapter 6

The Vision: The Three Levels Of Being

Michelle introduced me to meditation via the Self-Realization Fellowship temple in Eagle Rock, California.[7] I don't know how it worked; I just know I felt calmer and more peaceful when it was a part of my daily routine.

In the beginning, I had to meditate every day to feel its effects. Then after a few months, I could get away with meditating every couple of days, then once a week, and then once a month.

What I am about to share here, I was advised to leave out of my first book, *The Infinite Now*. I was told no one would believe it: It might make me sound crazy and possibly undo any credibility I had. Yet, in this second book, I am throwing caution aside. You can blame Dr. Elisabeth Kübler-Ross for this. I read somewhere that Dr. Kübler-Ross, the renowned psychiatrist who penned the widely accepted Five Stages of Grief theory, was advised by her editor not to publish her Near Death Experience (NDE) research collected from four decades of working with dying patients, lest it diminish her academic credibility.

It was only in her later years that she shared her life-after-death research. In one amazing story, she described a client's strange visit. The visit was strange because Mrs. Swartz (her client) had died ten months prior yet now sat in her office urging the doctor to continue her life-after-death research. She knew Dr. Kübler-Ross was discouraged and close to quitting, as this research was not well known or accepted at that time.

Dr. Kübler-Ross was so astonished she asked Mrs. Swartz to write a note as physical proof she had been there. Mrs. Swartz wrote and signed the short note and left it on her desk. Shortly thereafter, she disappeared into thin air, but the note remained. That note helped Dr. Kübler-Ross believe all the unbelievable occurrences she was witnessing and served as a constant reminder to soldier on with her research. This is not a story a credible and respected psychiatrist usually shares,[8] and her example inspired me to set aside fear or any need for credibility and just say what I wanted to say.

As a side note, I feel like Dr. Kübler-Ross assisted me as I wrote this chapter. I was looking for this story to cite and could not find it anywhere on the Internet. I bought her books on death and dying but could not find it in those books either. I also bought her memoir on Kindle, only because I thought it would be an interesting read. After searching everywhere without success, I was going to remove this story because I could not find proof it ever happened. Then, when I was working on this chapter again, I had the urge to open her memoir and check once more if it was in there somewhere.

I had not yet started reading the book, so I was surprised when instead of opening at the beginning, the e-book opened to a page toward the end of the book. I started reading the page and realized this was the story I had been looking for. Coincidence? A 300-page book just happens to open on the very page I was looking for? I'd like to think she wanted the story included here and gave me a helping hand from the other side.

It was during this heavy period of meditating that I would sometimes receive messages. I don't know the source of these messages, but they were often helpful and profound. Let me explain how I received these messages because the subtle nature of the communication is not like normal conversation. For me, the messages would appear like a sudden download of what I can only describe as a complete unit of information that was suddenly in my head. It was usually random, having no relation to anything I was thinking.

If I did not write it down immediately, it would float away like an ethereal mist. *I learned from a channeler friend that you know the message is not coming from your own mind if it dissipates right away and that messages from the ego-mind are more persistent and nagging.*

During one meditation, I was shown what was called the "Three Levels Of Being." The information was simple, but at the time, incomprehensible to me. They are:

Level 1: Victim
Level II: Empowered
Level III: Surrender

I did not understand why there were only three levels nor what they meant. I knew I did not like the third level. Surrender was the enemy of my greatest love, control. Surrender sounded to me like a disaster waiting to happen.

It took many years for me to finally realize the levels represented a rough model of our spiritual evolution. And, by spiritual evolution, I mean one's increasing ability to navigate life's obstacles while maintaining inner peace. These levels represent the three perspectives from which we respond to our everyday occurrences.

I also realized we don't travel through the levels in a steady upward trajectory. Instead, we jump between the levels, just as our emotions can span a wide spectrum in an instant. For example, on a good day, we might respond from a Level III perspective, i.e., with patience, compassion, and trust. But when hungry and jet-lagged, or depressed and fearful, we might respond from a Level I perspective, i.e., with anger and blame. The goal was not to respond from one perspective all the time but to be aware that there were different perspectives from which to perceive and respond to life's events.

Level 1

Level I is characterized by the qualities of victimhood. To the victim, life just happens seemingly at random. From this perspective, there is no perceived control or responsibility for any aspect of life. People from this perspective complain a lot. Everyone else is to blame for all the good and bad that happen.

From this perspective, there is no awareness that thoughts have an energy field. From this assumption, there can be no realization that repetitive thought patterns create strong energy fields that, over time, become dense enough to materialize as physical matter. Change from this perspective is difficult at best, as this person has cut themselves off from the very energy source that can effect change. It is the equivalent of needing to travel in a car that has no gas and no driver.

People at this level tend to criticize and judge others. They do this to create the illusion that they are "greater than". If everyone around them is "less than", it gives them an illusion that they are better. This, however, effects no real change or lasting feelings of adequacy.

Level II

Level II, Empowerment, is characterized by the qualities "creation" and "free will". At the second level, there is an awareness that thoughts have an energy field that acts as a building block for their reality.

Empowered with this knowledge, people at this stage realize they can create health, wealth, and happiness if the right elements are present. (Obviously, this is a simplified version of the manifestation process, which I have explained in greater detail in *The Infinite Now*.) The very short explanation is that knowing, rather than believing, in the existence of something creates a stronger energy field for its creation. If there are no contradicting conscious or subconscious thought patterns, the energy field can materialize into physical reality faster. Competing and conflicting subconscious thought patterns, life lessons, and other factors are reasons why thoughts don't always manifest in our daily lives.

People at this level have an agenda and use a disciplined mind to harness energy to fulfill it. And, while thoughts do not materialize immediately, they do build up enough energy over time to materialize as physical matter.

Unfortunately, some have taken this too far, causing people to believe that everything that happens is a result of their thoughts. I cannot tell you how many of my clients had told me how heartbroken or angry they felt when they received a cancer diagnosis, only to be told by a well-meaning busybody that they created it.

What I am most clear about is that we don't know everything about the manifestation process, and we don't know why certain life events happen. In many spiritual treatises, it is explained that souls choose certain experiences for the spiritual growth they will afford.

The honeymoon period of discovering the power of the mind is eventually followed by disillusionment and disappointment when one experiences an unexpected traumatic event that could not be prevented, removed, or controlled with the mind. When faced with overwhelming circumstances, the person is often ready for Level III.

Level III

Level III is characterized by the quality of "surrender". At this level, the person has let go of the figurative steering wheel and trusts the will of God (or whichever higher power you believe in) to handle the particular life circumstance. Picture driving up an icy, curved, and steep mountain road, at night, during a blizzard. You have the choice of driving to your destination yourself or having a seasoned mountain driver take the wheel while you relax in the passenger seat. Personally, I'd feel safer letting the experienced driver take the wheel.

Level III requires trust. We trust because we don't see, from our limited perspective, how this event fits in the greater scheme of things. For example, if one had no experience in weight lifting, they wouldn't know the pain after a session is the muscle tearing and rebuilding itself into stronger, bigger muscles. Similarly, a higher perspective affords greater knowledge, just as hindsight is different than knowledge in the moment.

Surrender at this level does not mean one has relinquished all control or goals in their life. It's not a directive to give up all goals, desires, or preferences. This level is not a resignation, so much as an elevated spiritual perspective.

This feeling of peace comes from knowing that whatever happens on the small scale of our lives is leading us toward a spiritual destination we can't see or understand. There is no final destination but an infinite expansion of energy that never ends. We are part of, and perpetually connected to, an infinite energy field. The whole point of our time on earth is to realize this truth.

The stories herein can loosely be categorized within these three levels: 1) stories in which I chose negative thoughts, felt stuck and powerless, and full of anger and blame, 2) stories in which I discovered the many facets of energy, and how we are living energy antennas capable of sending, receiving, and blocking energy, and, 3) stories in which I discovered the omnipotent power of surrender, i.e., give up control, gain the kingdom.

These realizations were coming on like rapid-fire, which my husband confessed later, made him feel uneasy. I looked the same on the outside, but nevertheless, I was different. He didn't know how to relate to this new person, and he wanted back the lawyer he married. His reflexive response was to mock, insult, and cross-examine everything I did or said. I felt as if the one person in the world that was supposed to have my back had become my enemy.

This was a source of deep sadness.

Chapter 7

The Monster In The House

My husband and I made the practical decision to have our second child 20 months after the first child, solely because the obstetrician was added to our medical plan. I started to doubt this sage decision when literally everyone around us started asking, "Why are you having the kids so close together?" or commented, "Well, bless your heart, you guys are ambitious." Looking back, having two children in diapers was probably ill-advised.

I missed work. I missed wearing a suit, going out to lunch, and feeling accomplished. No one warned me of the price of becoming a stay-at-home mom. Now I had no power. I was one of the kids asking permission to buy anything or to go out to eat or to go anywhere. I felt isolated, depressed, and very lonely.

I was in between worlds. I no longer fit in with my work friends, and the other moms judged and distrusted me. I was one of those career types, merely visiting the sacred territory of the "stay-at-home-mom". No one was interested in bonding with someone who would be going back to work.

And, I had a terrible secret: I was really a monster. At least, that is what I thought about myself. I pictured all the other moms having blissful days with their children—learning, laughing, and bonding. I, on the other hand, woke up every morning scared to death that this was the day I would lose the battle with my inner rage. Today I would lose control of that wave of intense energy and hurt one of my kids.

I did not realize I had this problem with anger until I became a stay-at-home mom. As a child, I was not allowed to express any anger. If I mimicked my mom's behavior and raised my voice or slammed a door (I did not even consider striking back), I was slapped hard across the face (a violent, humiliating experience) or rabbit punched or kicked. Instead of being protected or supported, I got helpful warnings from my dad to avoid doing anything that might make her mad. This, I realized, resulted in angry energy being suppressed deep within me.

Notwithstanding my early childhood, my mom was not a one-dimensional rage-filled parent all the time. In my early adult years, she apologized and applauded me for not following in her footsteps when I became a parent. In subsequent years, she became a very supportive, generous, and loving parent. Having not been in a Japanese Internment Camp for three years, from age 3 to 8, I cannot know how that experience might have sparked rage and affected her future parenting.

Now, as a stay-at-home mom, I had long silent hours, and I could feel that suppressed rage resurfacing. I was always thought of as the "nice one", "so peaceful and kind". I was actually able to keep up this facade for decades until now. A toddler will push your buttons unlike no other. I felt like a fraud. Nice on the outside, dark and evil on the inside.

They say that the difference between rage and anger is anger discharges when you express it. Rage, on the other hand, does not discharge until you harm your "target". I lived this distinction every day, and I knew from personal experience it was true. So far, I had won this battle, but it was exhausting and scary, and I felt guilty and ashamed. I felt so much rage at my two innocent, beautiful children. I casually mentioned to my husband one day, "Is it normal to feel like throwing the kids against the wall?" I was surprised when he responded, "Yes. The difference is you think it, but you don't do it." But, I knew the rage in me was not normal. It felt like a coiled spring, ready to explode.

I had stayed in contact with my work friend Michelle after I left the firm to become a stay-at-home mom. She called me one day, really excited about this woman she met at this spiritual event hosted in Los Angeles called the Whole Life Expo. Spiritual teachers and practitioners from all over the world attend this annual event, sharing their philosophies and publications and performing demonstrations of their healing modalities.

Michelle told me that she had met a woman named Christina Thomas Fraser, who wrote this book I *had* to read entitled *Secrets*.[9] This woman did work called rebirthing, a breath session that supposedly released past emotional trauma. If emotional trauma is suppressed, then that stuck energy would cause fatigue, fear, and depression.

I felt skeptical about the book and the idea of rebirthing. How could you possibly shift physical anger with your mind? Wasn't the mind the problem? She explained that when you have stored anger or rage within you, keeping it down was like trying to keep an inflated beach ball under the water in a swimming pool. It takes all of your energy and attention and, if you aren't concentrating all your energy on it, it keeps bobbing back up to the surface.

According to her book (which I bought that same day and read in one sitting), emotional energy doesn't go anywhere and crystallizes, over time creating actual physical blocks within a person's energy body. This creates obstruction, slowing or preventing energy from freely flowing. And because energy is the source of everything, free-flowing energy births creativity, well-being, and prosperity. Then I read something in her book, which surprised me. Apparently, what we think of as random life events are actually experiences our bodies create to offer opportunities to feel those suppressed emotions and release them.

That was all I needed to hear. All my feelings of rage, fatigue, and depression suddenly made sense. I wanted this stuck energy out of me, *pronto*. When I called the number on the back cover of the book, I couldn't believe I got Christina on the phone straight away. I was telling her how I found out about her and how I was really interested in getting a session. Yet, I wasn't sure how I would see her since she lived in Encinitas, which was a couple of hours south of me. There was also the childcare issue; I did not have a regular babysitter. Both my husband and I did not have family living in the area, and both of us felt hesitant to trust strangers.

During this conversation, my husband started yelling at me to get off the phone. I nervously told her I had to go, but something in my voice touched her heart, and she told me she would drive up to see me. Better yet, if I found a couple more people to do sessions with her, she would not charge for the travel up to my area. Grateful, I hurriedly told her I would make it happen and would be in touch.

Chapter 8

A New Reality

After several phone calls, I set up a rebirthing session with Christina at Michelle's house. This would be the beginning of many things I would hide from my husband. Christina was beautiful, but not in the ethereal way I expected her to look. It was comforting that she wasn't wearing crystals and chanting "OM". She almost looked like a blond, blue-eyed businesswoman, but most importantly, she exuded an air of calm and kindness. There were four of us meeting at Michelle's house for rebirthing sessions with Christina.

Michelle went first. The rest of us sat in silence in her living room, not knowing what to expect. When she came out of the session, I looked up expectantly. She shrugged and said, "It was relaxing, but nothing much happened." I felt let down.

Then Christina turned to me, "OK, you are next," she said. "I will explain how the breathing is done, and then we will go into the back room." As she was talking, I suddenly saw a light behind her. It looked like a person but made of light. Christina stopped talking and asked, "Are you looking at my aura?" "No..."

I responded slowly. She smiled, "Oh, you see the spirit that works with me." Excuse me? The *What* who works with you??

I looked closer, and there was suddenly so much love beaming at me from whatever this was that, to my horror, I started to sob. And, I felt like a gazillion volts of electricity rushing up my legs. I felt scared and confused. I did not read about this experience anywhere in her book.

Christina jumped up, grabbed my hand, and pulled me to the back room. She explained later that I was having a spontaneous rebirth (when the process starts on its own). She stared at me, and I felt very self-conscious. Wasn't she supposed to tell me how to do this special breathing?

She gently pushed me back and told me to lie down. She said, "Breath, connecting the inhale to the exhale with no pause in between." I started breathing as instructed, and I could feel that electricity coming up my legs into my knees, and it hurt; a lot. The pressure was building in my knees, and the pain was almost unbearable. I was trying to understand how in the world, physical energy was flooding my body from some unknown source. "My knees hurt," I blurted out, barely able to contain my panic. She said, "I know. Your knee chakras are blocked, and I am clearing them right now." *Excuse me? My What are blocked?*

Whatever she was doing alleviated the pain. I could not see what she did as my eyes were shut very tight as if not being able to see would somehow keep out all the strangeness of this experience. Then I felt like a giant hand was squeezing me, all over my body, by some invisible force. My mind was trying to comprehend how this was possible. I had never experienced anything like this in my life. And then, I had this ridiculous thought, "Oh crap, my husband is going to kill me if I die on this woman's table."

The pressure kept building and building, and I felt like I was being literally crushed all over my body. "This hurts," I kept repeating. "It's OK," she said, "keep breathing. You are OK. I promise. You are re-experiencing your physical birth."

When I thought I could not take anymore, the pressure released around the crown of my head, then down my neck, shoulders, torso, hips, and finally, my legs. My arms and legs were bent and shaking, and much to my surprise, I let out a loud infantile cry. Part of me was watching and thinking, "This is weird."

Tears were streaming down her face as she held me, gazing lovingly into my eyes, murmuring, "You are a beautiful girl. I love you, and you are wanted." I realized she was reprogramming me by changing my birth experience. The room was buzzing with electrical energy, and there was a bright light permeating the room. I was in awe and could not move. I had to lie there for several minutes before I had the strength to sit up and walk back to the living room to join the others. I had no words for the experience. It felt like the most blissful, peaceful feeling I had ever experienced.

The next day, I had no energy. I called Christina, and she explained that I had been born and it would take a couple of days to regain my normal strength. She was right, and from that day on, my life was permanently changed. I now knew with certainty there was a force greater than ourselves, filled with the most incredible loving energy. I would feel that electricity running through my body from that day on.

A week after my session, I was put to the test. I had restored my kitchen chairs to their original cream color. The newly cleaned chairs stayed clean exactly five minutes before my toddler son spilled grape juice all over one of them. Did I mention it took six hours of scrubbing, and they were cloth-cushioned chairs? Normally I would have thrown a cartoon-like tantrum with my head ballooning out, eyes bulging, screaming at the top of my lungs, "What are you doing? Are you @#!!! kidding me?!?!"

Instead, I took a breath, and a thought instantly came to me, "What the heck was I thinking handing a toddler grape juice and seating him on cream-colored upholstery?" I was the @#@!! crazy one. I laughed out loud at the stupidity. Don't get me wrong, I still felt irritated. But for me, irritation was a huge improvement over the meltdown I would normally have had over such an incident.

Now, equipped with the breathing technique Christina taught me, I was able to move through the irritation quickly. I would not even recognize myself several months later and would continue with this process over the next ten years. What this gave me was hope, where before, there was resignation, shame, and despair. I have deep, deep compassion for those marinating in their own rage and the knowledge there are ways to soften and release this stuck energy.

In the months to come, I would discover releasing stuck trauma energy had other side effects I hadn't expected.

Chapter 9

The Hot Tub Incident

I was in the hot tub with my rebirthing instructor, Christina Thomas Fraser. This was my second session. Christina explained that the warm water simulated the uterine environment and might stir up in-utero memories. She handed me a snorkel mask and breathing tube and explained I would merely float on the surface of the water and breathe through the tube. Because this type of session was more intense than "dry sessions", she said we would only breathe for ten minutes and not the usual sixty minutes.

I recall putting on the mask, dipping my face in the water to make sure it was airtight, and then starting to breathe through the tube with my legs resting on the hot tub floor. The last thing I remember was the hollow, echo-like sound of my breathing in the plastic tube. I don't recall how this happened, but Christina said that after a few minutes, I sunk to the bottom of the hot tub, fully submerged, and remained there for what seemed like a long time.

Concerned for my safety, she slid her arms under my armpits, slowly brought me back to the surface, and looked into my eyes to make sure I was okay. Assured I was fine, she lowered me back under the water, where I remained for the rest of the breath session.

I had the most extraordinary experience. When fully submerged, I felt very peaceful, with no need to breathe air. I immediately noticed a baby boy with its back to me, arms crossed in anger. I said (telepathically), "Hello," and the baby continued to ignore me, obviously very angry with me. I felt confused. Who was this baby, and why was he angry?

Then he said, with his back still turned toward me, "You got rid of me and then acted as if I never existed." My mind was trying to comprehend how this was possible. Why was I fine under the water, and how was I seeing this little being? Then I realized this was the being that was terminated when I was 17. Inexperienced and ignorant, I was the cliché girl who got pregnant after her first time having sex.

He was right. I did pretend he never existed. It was too painful to acknowledge that I was a murderer. The fact that I had killed someone took away a lot of judgment I may have had toward others. It was a source of unbearable pain, and I guess I pushed that memory far under the surface of my awareness.

I paused and poured out all my regret and shame to the little boy for never acknowledging his existence. He must have felt the weight of my deep-felt sorrow and finally turned to face me. I don't remember what we said after that, but he did end up in my arms, and we remained in a silent embrace for a long time. At some point, we said our goodbyes, and I floated back to the surface.

After that experience, I felt a heaviness lift from my chest, a heaviness I hadn't realized was there. I had made peace with the past and could move forward with compassion for my 17-year-old self.

When we spoke of it, Christina explained that when people enter a different "dimension", they no longer need to breathe. I did not understand what she meant by dimension, but I did feel as if I was in another world; peaceful, light, and timeless.

This was my first experience of being in "another dimension." Later, as a practitioner, I would witness many clients go to other dimensions during their breathwork sessions. They would experience everything from meeting Jesus to traveling to a scene from their childhood to just feeling like they were in another place that felt peaceful and still. All would report that they didn't need to breathe in this place they were visiting.

A few years later, I would visit a rebirthing training to be a guinea pig for the trainees. During the breathwork session that day, I would again move to another dimension, and the trainees would all notice I was not breathing for a long period. This was a dry rebirth session (which means lying on the floor, not breathing in a hot tub). I remember in that session, I saw a flower with a gazillion petals. It felt beautiful and peaceful, but I didn't know what it meant. Years later, while meditating in a temple, I noticed a painting on the altar that looked identical to the flower I saw in that rebirthing session. It turns out that the flower was the Thousand Petal Lotus, a symbol of spiritual enlightenment. It was experiences like this that made clear there was so much I did not know or understand about our world.

Chapter 10

The Swamp Full Of Alligators

After that second rebirthing session with Christina, I attended one of her week-long intensives. It sounded like one of those *kumbaya* huggy-feely workshops, so I was unprepared for this spiritual boot camp. That week was exactly like its title: *Intense.*

When you are in a roomful of people committed to confronting their suppressed emotions and memories, the interaction gets real in a way that feels chaotic. And, I guess that is the point. Yet, in a society where people rarely tell the truth and hide behind frozen smiles that don't reach their eyes, it's foreign and a bit terrifying when telling the truth, and nothing but the truth, is the new normal.

Christina explained that the energy would intensify and that at times we may start to cry uncontrollably, but we were not to suppress it but rather feel the strong emotions and keep breathing. If the wave of emotion(s) got too intense, she instructed us to flag an assistant who could support us through the episode.

She said, "Before you speak, I want you to ask yourself, am I seeking attention or approval by this communication, and if the answer to either is yes, please refrain from speaking." I immediately quipped, "Well, I guess you won't be hearing from me this week." I was basking in the predictable laughter when I realized to my horror that I wasn't able to follow her instructions for even one second. Crap. How humiliating it was to be so transparently needy.

After more preliminary instructions, she wanted to shift the energy from our heads to our hearts and had us stand in a circle, where she handed out lyric sheets and played a song to follow along aloud or silently. My eyes were rolling inwardly. I hated this kind of crap. I was trying not to judge the process and this workshop when I felt this strong wave of emotion build in my chest.

Oh no. Not now. Not so soon. I didn't want to be the first one, but I couldn't control it, and before I could stop it, I was sobbing uncontrollably. WTF. I knew she warned that this might happen, but it was still embarrassing to be the first one. I felt exposed, naked, and vulnerable. It was then I knew I was here for a reason and would not let embarrassment keep me from any healing that could come from this experience. But this was still embarrassing, so I looked down and tried not to be such a spectacle.

I later learned my body was like an antenna that picked up any suppressed emotions. I often acted as a release valve of sorts. This was helpful in future rebirthing sessions when I suddenly felt strong emotions that weren't my own. This alerted me the client's body was trying to release suppressed energy, and when it couldn't, it would redirect that energy to me for release.

This phenomenon was agonizing at funerals if you can imagine.

Another woman asked to switch places with the woman next to me, and my new neighbor started to rub my back and coo soothingly. Whatever prompted me to cry stopped, and I was able to resume singing with the group.

When we sat down, Christina asked the woman who was originally next to me how she felt when the other woman asked to switch places. She admitted feeling angry and that she liked standing next to me. Christina then stated that there would be many times when someone might start crying and to leave them be. She explained, our instincts to soothe them out of the emotion may look kind but may not be as gratuitous as it seemed.

She said taking charge of their release process communicated that we felt we knew what was best and might also be motivated by our discomfort at seeing someone in apparent emotional distress. In other words, gratuitous acts, at least in this room, were not always gratuitous. It was just like opposite day. Feeling strong negative emotions was good, and comforting each other was bad. I started feeling very uneasy and vulnerable. My normal *modus operandi* of suppressing negative emotions, and forging ahead, did not earn you brownie points in here like it did in the outside world.

As the week progressed, I grew accustomed to the intense interactions. At times, it was so different from so-called normal life that I found it comical. At one point, one of the participants asked a question, and before Christina could respond, one of the other participants, a male therapist, decided he knew the answer and started lecturing the woman. (We were instructed at the beginning of the workshop that "side talk" was to be avoided and to direct all talk to the instructor at the front of the room). The woman's reaction was shocking, but secretly I felt elated by its raw authenticity. This was a real response with a capital R. She turned and roared at him with such intensity she became airborne, with her behind lifting off her chair three inches, legs jutting out rigidly, "SHUT THE FUCK UP! IF I WANTED TO HEAR YOU FUCKING SPEAK, I WOULD HAVE TAKEN YOUR FUCKING WORKSHOP." There was a shocked silence. Then she calmly turned back to Christina and said almost meekly, "Ok, I am listening." I was biting my lip so hard to keep from laughing I was surprised I didn't draw blood.

One point emphasized throughout the week was that there was no spiritual bypass. In other words, you could not ignore or repress the parts of yourself that you don't like. She emphasized that those parts you reject and suppress would become what she called our "shadows". Shadows are the negative aspects of ourselves that we cannot face, so we project those qualities on others. She said sometimes the shadows are so deeply repressed that they erupt as almost bizarre behavior when we least expect it. For example, one, who cannot accept his own homosexuality, might verbally attack those openly homosexual, accusing them of immoral behavior.

Shadows also surface when we judge people harshly with a lot of emotion and self-righteousness. The rule of thumb is the greater the emotion and judgment, the more likely it is a shadow. She coined the phrase,

"There is no way around the swamp full of alligators. The only way through the swamp full of alligators is through the swamp full of alligators." She meant ignoring, repressing, or denying disliked or rejected aspects of ourselves would result in suppressed energy, stagnation, and depression. The energy it takes to suppress that self-awareness would not only block our abundance, creativity, and connection with others, but it would also block our spiritual evolution.

That week I saw parts of myself that were painful to see. Throughout the week, Christina kept referring to me as this perfect mom, telling tale after tale about my two wonderful children. I could feel this energy building up again in my chest, and I worried it would erupt in an unexpected way sometime during the workshop. I felt like a fraud. Halfway through the week, I stopped another "super mom" story and said I had to say something about that. She looked at me quizzically and waited for me to continue. I could not look at anyone as I told a story I never wanted anyone to hear.

I told the story of the time when my son, Tei, was three, and after numerous instructions not to throw the ball in the house, he threw a baseball, breaking a window. I was not able to control my temper and slapped his little face. I can still see the three-finger marks on his smooth cheek and realized with horror that we were supposed to be at a birthday party in three hours. I felt like a criminal as he and I held the ice pack to his cheek, trying to make the marks disappear.

The external marks had been removed, but the internal ones remained as this normally goofy, fun-loving child spent the entire pirate party hiding under my shirt.

He was shy, scared, and completely thrown into a sea of hurt confusion that someone he loved and trusted so much had hurt him. I had never before hit him and would never do it again; the shame was so great.

After my "confession", many people in the workshop would not look me in the eye. Some avoided me altogether, and I felt nakedly evil. Not surprisingly, as the week continued and I forgave myself, everyone else in the workshop seemed to forgive me as well. It turns out there were many parents in the room with their own guilt over questionable past parenting choices.

I felt raw and vulnerable when I returned home. My husband and I had been growing distant for a long time. He would often say, "Everyone thinks you are crazy and should be put away." (I wanted to ask him who "everyone" was, but I suspected "everyone" was him, so I didn't bother.) I thought maybe he felt left out of this new world that was opening for me. I tried to see it from his point of view and thought maybe he felt excluded because I was no longer talking about much of anything with him these days, partly because all I got in return were mocking statements or outright insults.

I decided that night to open up and confess the things I had learned about myself during the workshop that I thought were contributing to the constant fights we were having. My heart sank when his response was, "You know you have too much time on your hands. You should do something more productive with your time instead of sitting around making up things to be upset about. What a self-indulgent waste of time."

The energy high from the workshop came crashing down. I felt crushed. And he planted a seed of doubt.

All night I tossed and turned, wondering if he was right. Was I really just a self-indulgent loser who needed to rededicate my time to something more worthwhile?

The next morning, I got a confirmation that felt like a gift from the heavens. My husband woke up and exclaimed, "Wow, I had a really weird dream last night." "Really, what did you dreamt?" I asked. He said, "I dreamt I had a job outside, like a construction worker. I was in this truck, and I couldn't go to work. I couldn't move forward or go anywhere because there were alligators everywhere, in the back of my truck, in the road, all around me." He then asked, "What's so funny?"

The part of the workshop that I hadn't shared with him was my teacher's phrase, "There is no way around the swamp full of alligators." It was this experience, and more like this, that would comfort and assure me I was not alone but surrounded by kind guides and beings sending me messages and reassurances.

Chapter 11

The YMCA Intervention

One huge turning point in this journey was meeting Elizabeth Terrel. It's funny how random decisions can become catalysts for the greatest transformations. One day, I made the decision to start taking yoga classes at our local YMCA. I had never taken yoga, but I thought it might help with my chronic shoulder pain. Little did I know that one decision would trigger a series of events that would end my life as I knew it at the time.

Back then, I was just beginning to learn that there was an energy field that ran within and around our bodies. I also learned that our thoughts, emotions, and actions had energy fields. I discovered that when what we think, do, and say are not in alignment, there are very real consequences that manifest as chronic pain or disease in our bodies.

I spent years doing things based on how I looked on the outside instead of how I felt on the inside. It began when I pursued a legal career to fulfill my dad's lifelong dream of becoming an attorney. He spent his life in service to his family and worked 35 long years as an accountant, a job he hated. Not surprisingly, he suffered from chronic sciatica pain most of his life, even after back surgery.

In college, I had no idea what I wanted to do for a living. Back then, people chose a profession and did it for the next fifty years. Changing jobs like you change your socks wasn't a norm. I figured the least I could do since I was undecided was to fulfill my dad's dreams. I worked hard to make him proud.

I was working so hard I had no time to think about how unhappy I felt. The law, while seemingly fascinating from the outside, can be an all-consuming career. Speaking from personal experience, I assure you that no amount of money or social status can make up for doing a job that doesn't light up your soul. Over time, a flat feeling of dissatisfaction will creep in as no amount of money or possessions can fill the hole or void that is felt within when one is not connected to their infinite energy self. I know. That was my life.

I did not know that our thoughts, feelings, and actions create three separate energy strands that, when not in alignment, can cause havoc in your body and your life. What this means is when you think "no", feel "hell no", and still say "yes", those conflicting energy strands will manifest measurable negative physical consequences over time. (Imagine the stress to your car if you drove it with one foot on the gas and the other on the brake at the same time.)

I did not know at that time that within the physical body was an energy body. This energy body has electrical lines (much like the electrical wiring in your house) that can get depleted, tangled, and disconnected. This has been documented in scientific research, and doctors now know that the location of that energetic depletion in the body becomes the eventual site for resulting pain and disease.

For me, this came in the form of chronic shoulder pain that would persist for more than 15 years. Because the source of this problem was energetic, no amount of massage, physical therapy, or muscle relaxants helped. After all those years, I was resigned to living with constant pain that made sitting, standing, or lying down uncomfortable.

I had heard yoga was helpful in resolving body pain, which is one reason I signed up for the YMCA yoga class. Despite weeks of shoulder stands and downward dog poses, my shoulder was getting worse, not better. One day in class, I spotted a new student. Her name was Elizabeth,[10] and her yoga poses were good, if not better than the teacher. She was beautiful, with short jet black hair and big, blue-green eyes. I was definitely fangirling this woman but felt too shy to introduce myself.

After the class, I was retrieving my children from the childcare center when Elizabeth appeared next to me to pick up her son, who was aged in-between my son and daughter. She introduced herself and suggested we sit in the courtyard and hang out while our children played together. This was the first interesting person I had met since agreeing to quit work and become a stay-at-home mom. I was fantasizing about our future friendship when she said, "I really like you. Too bad I am moving to San Diego next week."

I felt so disappointed that I barely heard anything else she said. But, I did hear her say she was enrolled in a two-year program called Quantum Energetics Structured Therapy™ (QEST), which was a type of energy healing. I had never heard of energy healing, so this information went right over my head, and I promptly forgot all about it.

About six months later, she called to tell me she was in the area and could she come by for a visit. Let's see, fold laundry, or visit with this amazing person? Decisions, decisions. When she arrived, she confessed, her purpose for coming to the area was specifically to see me. She said she hesitated to share the information, lest I think her weird or crazy.

She then shared she was having dreams about me. Dreams that showed her I was supposed to enroll in that two-year energy healing training called Quantum Energetics. Honestly, I was neither interested nor intrigued by this revelation. I told her as much and that I planned to dust off my dictaphone and return to practicing law once both children reached kindergarten.

Taking no offense, she asked if she could demonstrate the technique on me, during which the muscle testing (a test in which she pushes on my outstretched, rigid arm until the muscle weakens in response to an inquiry) revealed I had a thyroid problem (a goiter, or growth on my thyroid that my doctor noticed).

She also noted the nose job I had had as a teenager and incontinence that had been a problem since birthing those large spawns of my six-foot-two, German-Swedish husband.

Now she had my attention. How in the world did she know all that? She was clear. She was not diagnosing me but testing the electrical flow in my body, and that this was not some weird new-age ritual meant only for the psychically gifted. Anyone could do it.

I was fascinated, intrigued, and scared. Now I was faced with a real dilemma. I felt more drawn to this work than I ever had toward law. I gave myself permission during this hiatus from work to find my true life purpose. But, this was not the life purpose I was expecting. This was weird, strange, and well, weird and strange.

Despite this, I could not ignore the small voice whispering in my ear, "I think you should do the training. I think you should do the training." After she left, I was convinced this was destiny, this was meant to be, and that everything was now going to fall into place. Yeah, that's the way life works.

I was all amped up. I went into full-scale sales mode and told my husband all about this amazing visit. His strange reaction would be a precursor to all his strange reactions for the next ten years. He was skeptical, critical, and completely unmoved by any of it. In fact, his main concern was that I had not told him about the nose job I had as a teenager. He wanted to know what other skeletons I had in my closet.

Then his final reaction was, "No, I absolutely forbid it." Forbid it? It felt like an imaginary line had been drawn in the sand. He was forcing me to choose between our marriage or this training. I was shocked how fast I replied, "I think I may take the training."

Chapter 12

The Reading

The decision whether to take the QEST training felt agonizing. I felt frozen in place, unable to make the decision. I needed assurance if I was making the right decision. I contacted my old word processor, Michelle. She explained there were tarot cards that could tell me what decision would work best for me.

I had neither used nor heard of tarot cards. It turns out, though most people think of them as a parlor game, this divination system dates back to the 1400s, originating in popularity in Europe. It is one of five ancient divination systems widely used in the world today: Astrology, Numerology, I Ching, Runes, and Tarot.[11] Historical origins notwithstanding, my willingness to use a divination system, even an ancient one, hinted at how desperate I felt making this life-changing decision

Michelle told me the name of some traditional tarot cards many people use and a guidebook to enable me to interpret the message of the card layout. I went to the only metaphysical bookstore I knew in Pasadena, The Alexandria. I felt excited and a little apprehensive as

I purchased the card deck, the book, and a velvet purple drawstring pouch that fit the cards perfectly.

I did not open the deck or the book for several days. I think I was afraid the cards would tell me what everyone in my life was telling me; don't be crazy, don't be irresponsible, don't do something that in the end won't make as much money as law, and that will make your husband mad.

When I finally decided one day to go ahead and see what the cards had to say, something else happened that I was not expecting.

Though I tried to keep in touch with my friend JJ Rosetta (a lawyer I had met on a case), it was hard. She couldn't relate to my new world. When you aren't up to your eyeballs in potty training, feeding finicky eaters, and power struggles with headstrong toddlers, there is no common ground to connect. Our worlds no longer matched.

The point is, I hadn't spoken to her for months. I was still struggling trying to decide whether to upend my life and take the two-year QEST training. My heart was telling me, yes, but my fearful mind was telling me absolutely not.

This one morning, I decided to take matters into my own hands and give myself that tarot card reading. Go to the training, don't go to the training. I would leave it up to fate. I unwrapped the cards and set down the tarot manual. Suddenly, I had a thought float in. Give the cards to your friend JJ. I thought I must be imagining this, so I ignored that thought, but it persisted. Give the cards to your friend. Give the cards to your friend.

Now, I am not in the habit of receiving strange arbitrary messages about my friends, so I decided to do a small reading for myself to determine if this was a real message or if I was going crazy. Michelle had taught me how to ask yes or no questions with the cards. So I asked the cards, "Should I give JJ Rosetta (she liked being referred to by her whole name when possible) the cards, yes or no?" The cards said yes. I didn't like the answer. I mean, I just spent $65 on these brand-new cards, the silk pouch, and the manual. They were mine!

I asked again. Yes. I asked again. Yes. Then I had this thought. OK, if I am supposed to give her these cards, have her call me today. I barely finished having that thought when my phone rang. "Hello?" It was her. "What the hell do you want?" She laughed good-naturedly, asking, "What kind of hello is that?" I explained.

Silence on the phone after I finished. She then said slowly, "Did I ever tell you my mom read cards for the stars? Old-time stars like Dennis Weaver and such." "Really?" I asked. She went on explaining, "Yes, my mother used two types of cards, and when she died, she gave them to me."

It turns out that JJ Rosetta was an amazing card reader. The trouble was, she was also a devout church-going Catholic girl who felt deeply conflicted about her abilities. It seemed blasphemous to her. We had been friends for years, but she never once mentioned she had this hidden talent.

I told her I guessed the cards I bought and the manual and the pouch were for her then. I then asked her, no begged her, if she could please do a reading for me. I told her this would be my first reading experience and that I felt desperate. I didn't tell her my question because I wanted to make sure the answer was coming from the cards and not what she thought I wanted to hear.

I was impatient for the reading, so she came to my house the next day. We sat in the kitchen, and she had all three sets of cards on the table. She explained she would do a reading on the same question with all three decks, and then we would see what the cards had to say overall. To this day, I cannot believe how specific the answer was or that all three decks gave the same answer.

Each deck said the same thing. You are going into a new pioneering area of healthcare, and everyone in your life is against it. Everyone! Things will turn out in the end, and you will help many, many people in your later life. Your family, friends, and acquaintances will all come around, and your decision will be supported. Your marriage, however, may not survive this change.

I have to admit that without this reading, I don't think I would have had the courage to go through with this decision. I just needed some reassurance that I wasn't just being impulsive, selfish, irresponsible, and irrational, as my husband claimed.

The irony was that her reading enabled me to do something that would benefit her greatly later on. It's funny how things turn out. It is almost as if there is an invisible screenplay that we participate in, but like the movies, there are often unexpected twists and turns in the plot.

Chapter 13

Should I Stay, Or Should I Go?

Iknew six months into our engagement that something was not right. I kept waiting for him to realize it too, but as it turned out, his ability to stuff down his feelings was far greater than I had imagined. The image of the perfect couple walking hand-in-hand into the sunset was all he needed, and truth be damned.

Even two kids and sixteen years later, we still had everyone fooled. When the news of our separation hit the gossip trail, everyone was shocked. The thing is, I thought I was being kind staying with him when I was so deeply unhappy. Yet, as it turned out, that was not a gift but an empty box that hurt him far greater in the end.

There were three defining moments during that sixteen-year period when clarity stuck, giving me the eventual strength and courage to leave. The first moment was not so much a moment, but an eight-year phase, as my husband put it. I mentioned that I was really unhappy, and he said it was just a phase that all couples go through and that it would pass. He said we could revisit the issue in a year.

Not one year, but three years later, he urged that it was still a phase and not fair for the children to devastate them. After eight years, I mentioned again that I was deeply unhappy, and his reply shocked me. "Pretty long phase, huh?" I suddenly realized, to my horror, that he was going to keep this going forever because he was getting what he wanted, which was not necessarily me, but this perfect Norman Rockwell image.

The second moment of clarity struck when I was watching a movie, the title of which escapes me. The married couple had been best friends since childhood. The wife realizes she is gay and agonizes about hurting her husband, who she cares for deeply. He has had an inkling of this over the years but loves her very much. He says to her, "I want you to be happy, and I wish I was the one that made you happy, but if I am not the one who makes you happy, I don't want to be an obstacle to your happiness." As I heard those words, I realized he loved her deeply and wanted what was best for her, even if it meant it wasn't what he wanted. At that moment, I realized what I was experiencing was not true love but possessiveness and control. With this realization, I cried until the salt from my tears stung my face.

The third and defining moment came after I returned from a workshop in which they taught an energetic exercise demonstrating real power. In this exercise, one person stood with one arm outstretched to their side. That person was instructed to imagine energy running up their legs, up to their heart, and through the outstretched arm.

The instructor explained that when energy is run through that arm in that fashion, it is very hard to bend that arm. She even cautioned us to make sure the outstretched arm was not pointing at anyone, as in the past, while doing this exercise, people standing in the direction of that arm had been knocked to the ground. This exercise demonstrated that true power came from within and was not about money, physical strength, or other external representations of strength.

I was so excited about learning this that I taught both my mother and my ten-year-old son. When neither my mom nor I could bend his arm, I could see the delight and excitement in his eyes as he made this discovery. He could tell we weren't pretending and couldn't bend his arm.

When my husband came home from work, my son could not wait to show him his new discovery. I watched through the back sliding door as my son ran up to him excitedly and told him of his new discovery. Then I witnessed a 6'2" adult male exert all the strength in his body to force my son's arm to bend. My blood ran cold as I watched the light in my son's eyes dim and go out. With shoulders slumped, he walked slowly back into the house. (*Experiences like this one would teach him, for years to come, not to share these insights or discoveries with his father.*)

At that very moment, I realized that I had been beaten down mentally in the same way, day after day, year after year, and if I stayed in this house, I was telling my children this was acceptable. Not all beatings in a marriage are physical. Internal scarring is just as damaging until only the shell of one's former self remains.

Despite my resolve that day, I stayed out of fear and guilt. How could I break up my family? My teacher advised me not to take action unless I was absolutely sure what to do. She said, "Hold the tension until a resolution makes itself clear." The funny thing is that I held that tension for eleven years and developed hypertension in my body. I am convinced holding this tension was its source.

One day I said to my husband, in a very quiet tone, without anger or blame, "I think I would rather die in a cardboard box on the street than remain one more day in this beautiful house with you. I know that all the horrible things you say to me are coming from my mind because all the things you say are things I think about myself, but I just cannot live this way any longer."

His response surprised me. He said, "I am unhappy too. Let's go to counseling. (I had been asking for years for us to go to counseling). He then emphasized, "It's the least you can do, rather than devastate the family without even trying."

So, off to counseling we went.

Spoiler alert: It wasn't enough to save our marriage, and we ended up divorced anyway. Here is the paradox: On the one hand, I knew his hurtful words were repeating back to me the words in my own head, relentless and critical.

Yet, having been trained as a rebirther and knowing the common patterns people created from their birth and childhood, I also knew I had subconsciously married someone whose behavior mirrored that of my abusive mother in an attempt to heal emotional wounds from my childhood.

But the abuse here was confusing, to say the least. He wasn't an alcoholic, and he didn't hit me, so there were no clear signs of abuse. I did know how I felt... like a shell of the person I used to be. I felt beaten down, and worthless, and scared.

One day, a close, longtime friend called me. She had been in counseling for help with her relationship. Her counselor recommended she read, The Verbally Abusive Relationship.[12] She told me, "I could never understand your marriage until I read this book. This book is your marriage, and you should read it, like yesterday."

I bought the book. In the first pages, it listed ten examples of behavior that indicated verbal abuse. My marriage had all ten. That information was crucial for my understanding of what was happening. It was confusing because he started out so kind. I was that frog that started out in the pot of cold water that didn't notice the water was slowly heating up until the water was boiling, and I was used to it.

Even though he was not an ideal mate, he was and is an amazing parent. He understood his spiritual assignment and did it well.

I felt terrified to share this information, which felt so personal and vulnerable. I did so to help anyone out there who also feels "boiled" and might understand their situation better from knowing about this book because each behavior on its own is not problematic. It's the list combined that adds up to verbal abuse.

Chapter 14

The Question

I don't remember why I ended up in a solo session with the therapist one day; perhaps my husband had a court deadline or was in trial. I do know I dressed up for the occasion. Not fancy dressy, but dressy casual. I wondered if he could tell that I, in stereotypical fashion, had a huge crush on him. There is something just so irresistible about a man who is mature, kind, and attentive. I felt like a homeless dog, hungry for attention and affection.

In response to his "how are you?" inquiry, I started to share stories about all my recent adventures in the metaphysical world. I was not-so-subtly trying to intrigue him. I was in awe of this new world and was eager to share it with someone.

The therapist was usually pretty soft-spoken and didn't say much, so I was taken aback when in response to my playful banter, he asked pointedly, "Maile, what if you were just an ordinary housewife?" The question felt like a punch to the gut. I could feel my face turn red with embarrassment. I felt naked and quite vulnerable. I didn't realize at that moment that I would revisit this question many times in the future and that it would take years for me to fully understand the question and to answer it for myself.

Why did I need to be special? If I was special, would I finally be good enough? It felt embarrassing to be so obviously needy. Then I felt humbled. Then I was angry. Who was he to ask such a question? But, my gut was telling me that question was important. Somehow I felt that I could unravel the source of all my mental suffering if I could answer that question.

Chapter 15

The Decision

I could not have made the decision to enroll in the two-year QEST training, even with JJ's reading, if it were not for all the weird coincidences. For one, I needed my mom to watch the children once a month for four days. The training was located in San Francisco, where my parents lived, so she and I would trade places once a month.

The problem was she was still working as a public health nurse and did not plan to retire for another five years. It seemed like destiny, then, when her supervisor randomly offered her a 50 percent pension increase if she agreed to retire immediately. It was an offer she couldn't refuse.

But then she informed me that she was not interested in obligating herself to come once a month to watch the kids. She said, as a retired person, she wanted to take classes and feel a sense of freedom with her schedule. I understood her feelings and did not press her or try to convince her to agree. I did have this calm feeling in my body that I would be in training, but I just did not know how that would happen.

The next two-year training was starting in September, and it was already August. Yet, for some reason, I still wasn't worried. I wasn't sure I was in the training yet anyway. I needed to fly to San Francisco to meet the teachers, Steve and Raedene VandenHeuvel. Coincidently, I was going to San Francisco to attend a friend's wedding, and it turned out that weekend was the only weekend, before the next training, that the teachers would also be in town.

I was told they interviewed potential students because they wanted to make sure you could handle the work. Because so many practitioners experienced results akin to miracles, they wanted to make sure as a practitioner, you had life experience and spiritual and personal maturity. They were also clear that they absolutely did not want any of their practitioners going on Oprah trying to get famous.

Their advice was always, do the work quietly and stay under the radar. The healing modality worked so well they worried we would be targeted by those who couldn't understand or felt threatened by this unconventional mode of healing. *Over the years, as energy healing became more prevalent, they were more flexible about this, but not by much.*

I met them at a restaurant for lunch in Half Moon Bay. The interview seemed casual. I felt like we were all just having lunch together and socializing. By the end of the lunch, my anxiety got the best of me, and I just had to know if I was accepted into the school or not. When I asked when I might find out if I was accepted in the class, the teachers glanced at each other as if to decide whether to tell me something.

Then they said it was really not an interview. They knew I was supposed to be in the class (just like Elizabeth), and meeting me was just a formality. I had to get used to people that operated instinctively instead of mentally. It was fascinating. Then they said I would experience many obstacles going through the two-year course, some of which may threaten my chances of graduating. It was not me in particular, they explained, but everyone that went through the training endured hardship along the way. They weren't sure why this was the case.

As it turned out, they were absolutely right, but I am getting ahead of myself. They said the class started not in September as I assumed but later that month in late August. They said I had until then to decide. I was sure I was supposed to be in the class, but my husband had forbidden it, and my mom was still not on board. But, I did not hesitate when I blurted out that I would be there in August to start the program.

As if to make this as dramatic as possible, my mom called a week before the first day of class and said she decided she wanted to help me make this happen. She said, she was bored and would welcome the chance to visit her grandchildren once a month. In fact, she said it was perfect as Dad, also retired, was driving her nuts. She was not used to their being together every day, all day.

Looking back, that was a magical time for everyone. She had a smoother transition into retirement, and my children spent many hours of quality time with her, which built a close bond they enjoy to this day.

Part II

The Extraordinary

Chapter 16

Down The Rabbit Hole:
A QEST Begins

On the first day of class, Raedene asked all of us to introduce ourselves and state why we enrolled in the program. There were only eight students, which surprised me. I was told the training was initially offered to nurses and doctors (Raedene had been an emergency nurse for 30 years), as well as others with acceptable licenses such as acupuncturists and chiropractors. But the medical industry showed little interest, so they opened the training to laypersons. And, because the training used medical school anatomy books, and because this training was no walk in the park, even the expanded enrollment yielded small attendance.

The first woman to speak was a short, stout, very serious former emergency room nurse of 40 years named Mary. She had suffered a stroke five years before, during which she was not able to speak, that is until she had her first Quantum Energetics session. Her speech was still halted and difficult, but by the time she graduated two years later, her speech was much improved.

If that weren't enough, her son had terminal arm cancer. He was actually the one who introduced Mary to the QEST™ work.[13] As a nurse who had worked in the emergency room for 35 years, Mary was very upset that her son was refusing traditional allopathic cancer treatments and even more upset that he was working with this woman quack. She asked to be present during one of his sessions, and thereafter, scheduled a session for herself. *The rest, as they say, is history.*

The doctors took x-rays and determined they needed to amputate his arm to save his life. But when they went in, cancer had spread so much they closed him back up, and informed him he had three months to live, and advised him to get his affairs in order.

With no other options, Mary's son kept getting sessions with his practitioner, Paula Martin Burns.[14] When they took x-rays again, the tissue that was formerly cancerous tested normal. On that day of the class, her son was still around, cancer-free. *I would find out during the training and my practice that these occurrences were normal. The cancerous tissue did not disappear but would test normal following QEST treatments. However, if the QEST treatments commenced when the cancer was too far advanced, it would not help the client resolve it.*

When it was my turn, I realized I had no miraculous story to share. In fact, the chronic shoulder pain, with which I was struggling, continued to hurt as I was going through the program. I would arrange child care, then drive to San Diego for the day, and buy as many sessions as Elizabeth[15], my practitioner, could do before I needed to drive back home. The frustrating thing about this program was the sessions were not tailored to target specific symptoms and resolve them.

The program was designed to unblock stuck energy within the body's meridian system, and by doing that, restore the body's innate self-healing abilities. Unlike other modalities, once a session was completed, it did not have to be repeated. If the pain were resolved, it would usually stay resolved, rather than the person having to come back each week to retreat. *As I went through the QEST program, my shoulder pain would resolve and remain pain-free.*

During this first class, I said I didn't know why I enrolled but that I knew I was where I was supposed to be. I also shared my hope that I wouldn't regret my decision, as this training was affecting my family and my finances in a significant way. Several students were nodding in agreement as I said this.

Later that night, I went to dinner with Elizabeth and two other women from her class. I was starving and anxious to order when one of the women said she saw two entities at the table. I saw nothing and thought, "I don't have the patience for this." The two women closed their eyes and "escorted" the entities to what they called the lighted bridge to the other side. They explained that some souls get stuck in between our world and the next dimension. They opened their eyes and said they needed my and Elizabeth's help. "Ok," I thought. Now they wanted group participation in their little "I see dead people" drama? I was probably hangry, but I felt annoyed and was questioning whether I could stomach this wacky lot for two whole years.

I assured them that I could not see dead people or entities, never had, never will, and could not be of any assistance. They said, "Just try. Close your eyes, and just show them the bridge of light, and they will follow it to their next destination."

Thinking that if I pretended to help, we could get to ordering faster, I closed my eyes. I was startled that I could immediately sense something or someone standing behind me. That freaked me out. Then I did see something in my head. It felt like my imagination, but there was a lighted bridge in the distance, and there were not just two but literally hundreds of "souls" running toward the bridge. I couldn't believe how many there were and that I could see them.

When they were all gone, I opened my eyes. I said nothing, as I still thought it was probably my imagination. One of the women, who had been silent until now, asked, "From where did all those people come? There were hundreds of them." I blurted out without thinking, "I saw them too. Hundreds." The first woman smirked and said, "This coming from the one who never sees anything."

That night, in our hotel room, I asked Elizabeth if she saw them too. She said not only did she see them, but that a couple more followed us to the room. I had sensed that too but was trying to ignore it because now I was scared. What crazy, sixth-sense nightmare of a Pandora's box had we opened? I had no desire to be followed around by dead entities. She said when they sense there is someone who can see and help them find the bridge of light, they gravitate to them. She said I could be doing this all day, every day, if desired.

I begged her to please make them go away. I was not interested in giving ghostly tours around the clock. She agreed. We didn't know what to do, so we prayed for assistance. It took several hours for them to get the message, but we just ignored them. I found out if you just ignore them, they go away. I guess dead people are no different than living ones. No one likes to be ignored.

Chapter 17

Energy Healing Works:
or I'll Trade You A Reading For
Some Grapefruit-Sized Cysts

The training was organized into three categories (1) instruction, (2) testing, and (3) practical application (working on each other, friends, family, and volunteer "clients"). Once a month, we would arrive on a Thursday night and take a test. Friday and Saturday, we received instructions about the work. Sunday, we had a day off, and Monday and Tuesday, we worked eight hours each day on people from the local community. These volunteer practice clients were charged a nominal amount, and during the two-year training, these monthly clinics took them through the entire program.

The work was called Quantum Energetics Structured Therapy or QEST (pronounced Quest). The word structured was included because it was a program with a specific progression from beginning to end. On average, it took between fifteen and twenty sessions to get a client through the program. The length of the program varied from client to client, as each person's energetic repair requirements are as varied as people themselves. In general, middle-aged women usually require more sessions, and teenage boy athletes the least.

Based on a model similar to acupuncture, in QEST, the body is believed to have energy lines that drive energy to the body's cells, tissue, and organs. If those lines become damaged, inadequate energy is delivered and, in turn, disrupts the body's proper functioning, resulting in pain and illness or disease.

The purpose of the work was not to remove or address specific symptoms or physical complaints. This work methodically went through the energy lines to remove blocks or damage, to restore the body's innate ability to heal itself. In the program, the body is organized into thirteen areas. Think of those 13 areas like 13 rooms in your body. The practitioner checks the electrical lines in each "room" to make sure the electrical lines in your body are working properly (i.e., that each room is connected and is able to transmit energy).

If the practitioner finds an energetic disruption, this is corrected by adding energy to specific points in the body where it is needed. This is done via muscle testing (to find the depletion points) and is performed by simply placing the fingers on the specific body point and directing energy for a specific time period, usually between one to three minutes.

The unique feature in this program was an energy correction rarely required repeating. Once the energy correction was done, you "programmed" the correction. *My son would call this "locking it in". Once I forgot to "lock-in" a correction, and he never forgot it. For years, he would constantly ask, "Did you lock it in?"*

This protocol of tapping in codes, muscle testing, doing energy corrections, and then "locking it in" was how the work progressed through the 13 sections or areas of the body.

The most frustrating part of this work was not being able to do codes out of order, especially when we thought it might help the client right away. This is hard to conceptualize, but picture a room with no walls. It would be hard to install a ceiling without the walls to hold it up. Much the same, when energy codes of a lesser frequency are not in place, higher frequency codes do not have the support they need to stay in place.

For example, let's say a client has lower back pain. There is a code that, when done, corrects disruption in the spinal discs. If you perform these codes out of order, the client may feel relief, but over time—like in days, weeks, or months—the pain may slowly return. It is always a struggle balancing the need to do the work in order with jumping around to get the client relief right away. Clients are asked to believe that healing their energy body, instead of getting rid of symptoms right away, will benefit them much more in the long run.

As a business model, this work did not seem financially sound. As practitioners, our work was designed to put ourselves out of a job. Since our primary goal was to restore the body's innate healing abilities, our clients' bodies were being energetically reset to heal themselves. Of course, there were exceptions to this model, i.e., if the person experienced a significant injury, such as a car accident, this would require energy supplementation via additional sessions. In this way, the work was not any more mysterious than giving someone air via CPR when they are unable to breathe on their own. One need not be psychic (although this ability we discovered would develop on its own as a practitioner worked with clients) to do this work. Just an open mind and an interest in helping people out of pain in a unique way are needed.

Our teachers were clear. We were not doing the work. We were merely acting as jumper cables to allow the body to start running more efficiently on its own. This was the blessing and the curse of this work.

In order to graduate, we were required to take ten people through the entire program. In doing so, the teachers said, we would have a word-of-mouth practice by the time we graduated.

I knew with whom my first practice session would be: JJ Rosetta. It was fitting she would receive my very first session since she gave me the intuitive reading that empowered me to make this vocational shift. She was very open to all things metaphysical, and though she was also an attorney, I knew she would not mock me for this new life direction. I was not prepared for what occurred when she arrived.

In the first session, there is a code for ovarian cysts that is listed in the QEST manual. It is checked on every client during their first session. The energy hold, according to the book instructions, is three minutes, but you are required to muscle test to make sure exactly how long to conduct the hold. When I tested the ovarian cyst code, my muscle testing indicated I would need to do three holds on her lower abdomen, one on each side and the middle area, for twenty minutes each.

I kept checking and rechecking the code because these holds were way longer than what my workbook indicated. She was also quite intuitive and picked up on my anxiety, and asked me if everything was alright. I asked her, "Do you have ovarian cysts, by any chance?" She laughed and grabbed my hand and plopped it on her abdomen, saying, "Do I have ovarian cysts?"

Underneath my fingers, I could feel a large grapefruit-sized lump. I asked her, "How long have you had this?" She nodded sheepishly and whispered, "Fifteen years." OMG. "Why didn't you get this checked?" I asked incredulously. She shrugged, "I guess no news is good news." I realized she was terrified this might be cancer.

I asked if I could touch the other areas where the holds were indicated. She agreed. I dragged my hand over her lower abdomen and felt not one but three large grapefruit-sized cysts. I placed my fingers on the first lump and sat down and tried to relax my arm so it didn't cramp during the twenty-minute hold. I was shocked but said nothing when I felt my fingers ever so slowly sinking as the cyst started to shrink. At the end of the twenty minutes, I could no longer feel the cyst. I stayed silent and continued to the next lump.

This second lump also slowly sank beneath my fingertips during the twenty-minute hold. During the first hold, I turned on the television to distract and entertain us. The third lump shrank to a third of its original size. *JJ would tell me the next morning the third cyst was also gone. She would also say that during those fifteen years, every time she stood up, the skin would feel like it might tear from the pressure of those lumps. The next morning, a large expanse of wrinkled skin was hanging from her abdomen as a visual reminder that that abdominal space had been filled with matter the day before.*

When I was done, I asked her how she felt, and she said it felt like the pressure was less in her abdomen. No kidding. I told her I wasn't sure how this was possible, but the cysts had seemed to shrink during the holds. Just then, the flame of a candle I had lit in the room shot up two feet high, literally two feet. I shrieked, grabbed the candle, and ran to the kitchen. I put out the flame in the sink. I told JJ I was returning that defective candle to Target the next morning.

She laughed and said, "Do you really think the candle is defective? I think it's my mom." She and her mom had been really close, and her mom had passed. I actually believed her because I had no other explanation for what happened that day. It was easier to believe her mom had done the healing from the other side.

After working on those cysts, we could feel a hard shell covering her whole abdomen area. I did more holds on that area, and that hard armor dissolved. Then under that were several smaller cysts throughout her abdomen. All but one also dissolved during that five-hour marathon session. I was willing to keep going, and so was she.

We worked on the last cyst for the next four months. It would repeatedly shrink, then grow. I was getting frustrated, so I called Raedene, my teacher. She said the cyst was too big for JJ's energy to remove it. She suggested JJ get it surgically removed. I liked that about Raedene. Being a former nurse, she had no interest in demonizing allopathic medicine. Both had their roles in restoring health.

It turns out she was right. JJ had the surgery, and we found out that we were only working with the tip of it, like an iceberg under the water's surface. That cyst was actually ten pounds, like a large fetus, that went up into her chest cavity.

The next person I worked on was a bit of a surprise. My dad was not a fan of this wacky career detour. He had paid for my law degree and the right to brag about it to all his friends. This weird vocation was just embarrassing. So when he showed up to my first clinic and signed up to be a monthly volunteer participant, I was happy he seemed willing to find out more about this new type of healing.

On the first day, he predictably mentioned the sciatica pain that he had his whole life, even after he had back surgery. On his fourth visit, however, he pointed to his elbow and knee and said there was a pain in those areas.

I asked him the status of his sciatica pain, and his response was, "What sciatica pain?" "What do you mean what sciatica pain?" I asked. He replied that he forgot he had that. Raedene said this happened a lot. People's minds were programmed to forget about chronic pain, just like a mother immediately forgets the agonizing labor pains as soon as her newborn is placed in her arms. *I would witness this phenomenon often during the years I practiced. I never experienced as dramatic a healing session as I did with JJ in the coming years. I believe I was witness to that amazing healing, to give me irrefutable proof that directed energy had the capability of effecting physical change. It was that experience that made me more receptive to all the other head-scratching phenomena that would follow.*

Chapter 18

Boundaries And Other
Healing Stories

I remember my very first clinic. As I placed my fingers on the woman's nose, I felt grief overcome me. I thought I might burst into tears. Not understanding what was happening, my butt cheeks clenched as I fought the wave of sobbing that was threatening to explode out of me. I found out later, this woman had septum correction surgery, and there was a lot of drama and pain surrounding the procedure. I guess when I touched her nose, it triggered that memory because I could see her shifting uncomfortably on the table.

She, too, felt a wave of emotion and suppressed it, whereupon that energy simply passed on to me. As soon as I finished working on her, I ran to the balcony, outside the work area, and promptly sobbed. As my crying was getting under control, I realized Raedene was standing next to me. She said simply, "If you cannot get better boundaries, you cannot do this work. In fact, it would be dangerous for you."

When I told her what happened, she explained that when I clenched my body, it trapped the energy in me instead of it passing through me. She said this phenomenon is why practitioners should not work on clients when they are depressed or sick. That weakness in our energy field makes us susceptible to picking up the clients' energy. She suggested, if that happened again, to relax my body and imagine the energy flowing through me.

Several years later, a fellow practitioner using another modality, NeuroModulation Technique (NMT), shared a similar story. His aunt was afflicted with cancer in her left eye. Her eye was the size of a golf ball. I am guessing his boundaries were not strong. After he worked on her, his own eye grew inflamed and swelled to the size of a golf ball as well. He freaked out and called his teacher, who explained the same thing that Raedene told me. It took a couple of days for his eye to return to normal. Energy healing is an art that must be respected and done with care and caution.

I also learned that children healed faster than adults and that the rule to do the work in order didn't apply to them—perhaps because their energy field is stronger and more flexible. My daughter had a best friend in elementary school whose mother was a surgical nurse. Her older sister broke her foot during a baseball game and would be out of commission for a month, according to her doctor.

At that time, I was still practicing with friends and family, and since this mother was a friend, I suggested that she bring her daughter to the house for a session. I still recall this mother sitting in a chair, arms and legs crossed, twisting her body into a pretzel shape. She was not used to this "out there" energy stuff and felt very uncomfortable. By this time, I knew I could do codes out of order on children. So I did the bone fracture code on her daughter, who arrived with a sock cast on her foot, hobbling on crutches. What I didn't know was that the next morning, her daughter woke up pain-free, put on her tennis shoes, and played baseball that afternoon.

My friend was freaked out but did not call me. She asked her chiropractor husband how this was possible. She asked her nurse colleagues if anyone had heard of this, but no one had. She did not speak to me for two weeks, but I did not notice. I called her two weeks later to ask if we were doing the usual Halloween pizza night at her house this year.

As we sat drinking wine and eating pizza, she told me what had happened after her daughter's treatment and confessed she had been freaked out. This would not be the first time this work would separate me from the other moms. Some were kind but cautious, like this friend. Some believed I was at best a witch, and at worst, a messenger of the devil. Fun times.

It was one thing when cysts you couldn't see dissolved under the skin's surface. But when I witnessed open wounds and burns instantly healing, it confirmed my belief that when energy is directed with intent, it can effect physical change. I found this fascinating.

I remember at my son's tenth birthday party when one of his friends stumbled over a lawn sprinkler and had a large gash on his leg. So deep was the wound, you could see the yellow layers inside his leg. Call it inexperience, but, in my newbie mind, I didn't question the healing technique for new wounds that the Pranic Healing teacher had mentioned in class. He was so confident in it that in previous classes, he cut himself in front of his students and then healed it right then and there.

I ran into the house for my workbook. Reading the page on open wounds like a recipe book, I waved my hand over the wound and followed the directions. The boy's friends were huddled around him and witnessed the wound start to dry up and close. Their eyes were round with surprise. I assured them they were witnessing this because they would do this and much more later in life.

In typical ten-year-old fashion, they leaptup and resumed playing, unfazed by this unusual occurrence. I, on the other hand, was in shock. I cleaned the wound and put a butterfly bandage on it. The following day when I was dropping that friend back home, his neighbor, whose daughter also attended the party, was watering his lawn. He glanced at me and said, "I am hearing weird things about your party." I chuckled and responded casually, "All lies," and drove off.

One day, my daughter spilled hot chocolate on her hand. It was burned pretty badly and was red, inflamed, and wet. I used that same fresh wound healing technique, and she and I watched as the burn dried up and healed before our eyes. She looked at me as if for an explanation. I told her it was like Harry Potter (her favorite at that time) and that we didn't need wands but could use our hands for energy healing. She seemed satisfied with that explanation.

I need to point out that in those days, I believed there wasn't anything energy work couldn't heal. Over the years, I learned that it didn't always work. I did not understand why it worked sometimes and not others. I do believe there is such a thing as beginner's luck. I think as a beginner, we don't know what we can't do, so our minds can't block our efforts. It is when the mind gets in there and starts questioning, doubting, and fearing that results start to vary.

I started learning things that the body did to protect us. For instance, when we have toxins floating about, our bodies will encapsulate those toxins and form a cyst. If the cyst remains and grows more toxic, it can transform into cancer. I think that is why some healers have discovered that simply detoxifying the body will allow it to restore health without medical intervention.

I recall one client who was going through the program. He did not mention the walnut-sized cyst on his back because he assumed there was nothing that could be done for that. After we did the session that had a lot of codes for toxins in various parts of the body, he arrived for his next session excited to share that that cyst on his back disappeared. He had it for five years, and it was getting bigger of late and painful. Following that toxin addressing session, he was in the pool with his girlfriend, and she noticed it was gone. I do believe that the body is an expert at knowing what to do with energy to maintain health.

After my dad's sciatica resolved, he was still on the fence about this new vocational direction of mine. He very much enjoyed bragging about his attorney daughter and was less thrilled about this questionable new line of work. I don't know why, but all of that changed the day I worked on his throat cyst. I was working on him in his bedroom (still just following the codes listed in the manual in order) when the code for vocal cord toxins came up.

Codes will test positive in three instances: when the energy is starting to build toward that condition, when the physical condition has begun to form, and when the physical condition has advanced more fully. I assumed my dad was coding for the vocal-cord cyst because the energy was forming, so I was surprised when I placed my fingers on his throat and felt a marble-sized round cyst.

I took his hand and placed it on his throat and asked, "What is that?" He startled and repeated my question, adding an expletive, "What the hell is that?" Ignoring his reaction, I did the hold and programmed it. By the end of the hold, the cyst was gone. A small flap of wrinkled skin dangled in its place. For some reason, this was proof in his mind that what I was doing worked, and he was suddenly on board with this strange life detour. *In fact, on my fortieth birthday, he wrote a long letter praising me for following my life's passion, acknowledging it took great courage and determination. Oprah would've been proud.*

I noticed that people either believed in the work without question, did not believe in the work without question, or thought that the work was of devil's origin and should be distrusted and feared. My husband was in the second and last category. It was getting increasingly more uncomfortable to be around him. He would ask me to hide my entire book collection in duffle bags under our bed when his parents visited. He would scowl and roll his eyes when children and parents from our son's baseball team would ask for healings during games.

For three years, I laid low. This baseball team had a lot of devout Christian families, and I did not want to take the chance our family was ostracized because of me. Then one day, during a tournament in San Diego, my son's best friend on the team was struck in the clavicle by a line drive and could not raise his arm. Tei stuck his head out of the dugout and pleaded, "Do something, Mom."

I motioned for this player's dad and asked him to follow me away from the field behind a shed. I did not want to draw attention. I explained to the dad that I did this type of energy work that lent extra energy, so his body could heal itself. This would not harm his son and actually may not do anything. This was the first time I witnessed that children don't need the work to follow the specific order, as I had been instructed. I did the clavicle code and told him to rest before the next game that afternoon at four. (It was 11 a.m. when I did this energy correction.)

Later that day, I was helping with dinner preparations, so I did not attend the afternoon game. My husband told me that when he returned to the field, the father ran to him and asked him to thank me. He pointed to his son, who was standing at the plate swinging at pitches. If you thought my husband would be pleased with this, you would be wrong. He found this all unbelievable and embarrassing. As word spread amongst the team members and their families, I became an unofficial team practitioner—all to the great irritation of my husband. This is why what happened one night perplexes me to this very day.

One night, I was sleeping in my son's room (not sure why) when my husband woke me up, telling me he had a really bad headache that wouldn't go away. He was wincing in pain. He asked me to work on him. I was sound asleep, so it took me a minute for my eyes to adjust in my workroom. When I glanced at the clock, I said, "Hey, it's two in the morning. Couldn't you wait 'til morning to wake me?"

His response startled me. He said, "I didn't think it would be fair for you to find me dead in the morning without giving you the opportunity to work on me." I thought to myself, "He must think this is really serious. I looked at his face, which was contorted with pain. When I checked codes that might cause this, the energy correction for brain aneurysm tested positive. As soon as I did the energy correction, his face immediately relaxed, and he fell asleep. *I know I said we weren't supposed to do codes out of order, but I felt panicked in this instance and did them anyway.*

I woke him up and escorted him back to bed. This time I slept next to him, keeping a close watch on him for the rest of the night. He was fine in the morning, and to my knowledge, did not experience this again.

Despite this experience and many others he personally witnessed, he continues to this day to refute any value of this work. I recall when my son had a tear in his shoulder ligament. This tear was confirmed in an MRI. Because this was a significant injury, my husband scheduled a second opinion and a second MRI with a more reputable orthopedic surgeon. I asked my husband if I could work on Tei before his second MRI, and he said it wouldn't change anything but the MRI couldn't be scheduled for a couple of weeks anyway.

I wasn't sure if two weeks was long enough for the shoulder tear to heal. I worked with my son doing all the corrective energy codes related to his shoulder. Then we waited a month until his consultation appointment. I worried that the two weeks after the energy work wasn't long enough for the ligament tear to heal before the second MRI. While we waited for the surgeon to appear, I asked my husband, could we please do a third MRI before we agreed to any surgery? I said if there were any out-of-pocket costs, I would pay for them.

His response was, "Ok, if you admit the work you do is worthless and ineffective." I was taken aback at this request but agreed quickly, "OK, my work is worthless and ineffective." I then asked, "OK, can I schedule the MRI?" He then said, "Not so fast. You also have to call up all your clients and inform them your work is worthless and ineffective." I was just going to tell him to shove it where the sun doesn't shine when the surgeon suddenly came into the room.

After introductions, he said, "Well, we have good news. The MRI doesn't show a SLAP tear[16] in his shoulder, but it does show some inflammation that we should keep an eye on. In any event, he should rest that shoulder for a bit before pitching again." *It is important to point out that the first MRI, taken before Tei received QEST treatment on his shoulder, did show evidence of a SLAP tear.* I kept looking straight at the doctor, not looking in the direction of my husband. We said nothing as we walked with Tei to the elevator. And, if you think this changed his mind about the work, you would lose that bet.

I have to confess, writing this chapter brought on a lot of anxiety. Raedene's warning not to make this work well known still rings in my ears. I am only doing so because energy healing is now more widely accepted, and I do believe people are ready to supplement their allopathic medical care with energy medicine. It takes a village, as they say.

I also have to emphasize that these stories notwithstanding, that no energy healing modality has solved the mystery of healing on command. Healing is complicated and mysterious, and I can't begin to understand all its nuances.

If you are curious about how healing works and how you might do it on yourself and friends and family, I wrote extensively about this topic in my book, The Infinite Now. *One thing that greatly affects the success of any healing is the body-mind connection. When I learned of this, it changed my whole world. It is a fascinating subject that one could study for a lifetime and barely scratch the surface.*

Chapter 19

The Body-Mind Connection

That honeymoon period of wonder and discovery was followed by frustration and failures. I would discover years later, after training in numerous healing modalities and looking for the infallible magic healing bullet, that the strength of my intent that was the strongest indicator for success. I could don imaginary goggles and shoot a neon pink healing gaze at my target and get the same healing success if I *knew*, not just *believed*, that the healing method would work.

That realization got me thinking. If the strength of my intent could effect physical change, what outcome would repetitive negative thoughts have on bodies and even lives? I started researching this question with all my clients, friends, and family and noticed a trend. Invariably, those clients that had the same negative thought (i.e., I don't have enough money) would all have lower back pain. Clients that had trouble speaking their truth would all have throat issues. One client, feeling financially impotent, got a nasty testicle infection.

Then, to my great surprise and delight, I discovered a book by Louise Hay, *Heal Your Body*. I was late to the "thoughts create life" game. Louise Hay not only discovered this truth, but she also wrote a book listing thoughts and their corresponding physical ailments. And, sure enough, low back pain was associated with thoughts of money lack. But she took it a step further. She included a diagram of the entire spinal column and, for each spinal segment, she listed a probable negative thought that might accompany it.

Today this is not a revelation, but 20 years ago, I thought I discovered the holy grail for healing. I began using this book to determine if pesky repetitive thoughts were a factor for clients that weren't shifting. Then I met Richard Skeie,[17] a friend of Elizabeth Terrel (both graduates of the QEST training). He wasn't practicing QEST much, as he believed thoughts and emotions were the core cause of all physical ailments.

I was fascinated when he told me that no fancy healing method was needed in awareness work. Just bringing the thought patterns to one's awareness and understanding their origins was enough to shift the energy and transform the person's physical state.

Our thoughts are so strong that they will affect, and can even change, our bodies. I experienced a remarkable example of this with a client. She was 5'10" and very slim. For some reason that I cannot recall, I asked her to imagine energy running through her body. I was waiting for her to complete the process when I saw what I thought was my imagination. Overlaid on her flanks were what looked like energetic saddlebags. I felt certain I was daydreaming, yet I asked her, "Do you think you are fat?" I was surprised, given her stature, when she replied without hesitation, "Yes."

Acting on instinct, I mentioned what I saw on her body. I was surprised when she sat up, mouth agape, and explained that she had just visited her mom two weeks prior, noticed her mother's saddlebags, and thought to herself, "That's me in twenty years." Trying to sound nonchalant but shocked at this very real demonstration that our thoughts generate energetic blueprints for our future, I responded, "Well, you are creating that reality as we speak."

If she did not realize her thoughts were creating a definite energy field, she would have started a 20-year journey toward that saddlebag reality and assumed it was an unfortunate gift from her genetics. What this experience taught me was how the energy generated by our thoughts, emotions, and beliefs builds over time and gradually impacts our realities. Thought by thought, the energy field grows stronger and stronger, taking your car down the road toward that eventual reality. Your car may detour at times, but energy acts like a homing device, recalibrating to that specific destination.

From this realization that thoughts are energy and repetitive thoughts eventually build enough energy to condense into our physical reality, I wondered what effect conflicting thoughts would have on our bodies. I also realized that thoughts were not the only thing that had an energy frequency. Our actions, emotions, opinions, and beliefs also had energy frequencies.

Upon further research, I realized that repetitive thoughts don't just collect in a linear fashion but multiply exponentially. For instance, picture a singer holding a single note and shattering a glass. That note has a specific frequency, and when held for a prolonged time, that frequency doubles, then triples, etc. The energy expands so quickly it cannot be contained in the glass, which is why it shatters.

Now picture your thoughts, emotions, and words as three separate energy strands. Someone asks you a favor, and you think "no", then feel, "hell no", then say, "yes." What effect does that "yes" have on your body? I think it is like putting your foot on the gas and the brake of a car at the same time. Eventually, your engine will burn out.

Over the years, I kept hearing stories that showed the effects of not speaking or acting upon your true desires. When I was agonizing over whether or not to leave my marriage, I mentioned to my teacher Christina that maybe I would wait until the children left for college. She cautioned me not to wait that long. She shared a cautionary tale about a close friend that waited until all her children left for college before freeing herself from an abusive marriage.

When the woman was finally alone as she desired, she was almost immediately diagnosed with advanced breast cancer and died shortly thereafter. Her energy was conflicted for so many years, and by the time she listened to her heart's desire, her body was in advanced stages of energetic conflict. I was already experiencing the effect of my internal indecision. I was "holding the tension" until I was sure what I wanted to do. Then I developed hypertension. Coincidence?

It was during this time of discovery that I learned that I might have a strong mental plan for my life, but another force was navigating my journey. One day, I was dropping off my son at kindergarten and noticed another mother I knew across the lawn. She looked different to me, but I couldn't quite put my finger on why. I promptly forgot about her and left to run errands.

Almost an hour later, at Costco, I was suddenly face-to-face with this parent. I said, "Hi," but then looked closer at her and said, "Wow, I have never seen that look on your face. You look terrified." She nodded in agreement, holding her breath. Suddenly I (the human antenna) started to cry. I asked her, "Are you trying not to cry?" She nodded vigorously. She asked for my business card and ran out of the store.

We arranged to meet at my house later that day. As she lay on my table, I realized her issues could not be addressed with QEST. She needed a rebirthing. I recalled how after my first rebirthing session, Christina mentioned that she thought I was going to become a trained rebirther. The mortified look on my face prompted her to apologize. She said she shouldn't have said that because I wasn't ready to hear that information.

It turns out that she was eight years too early with that little prophecy. Now, as I looked at this woman who really needed the work, I kicked myself. Why didn't I follow up with Christina and say I wanted to train with her? I hadn't talked to Christina in a long time and thought she had probably forgotten what she predicted and went on with her life.

Those days, answering machines were still a thing. After the woman left, I checked the answering machine. I was shocked to hear Christina's voice. She said, "Hi Maile. I was calling to say I was thinking about you today. I am doing a weeklong rebirthing intensive. I want you to be my assistant for the week. I will cover your food and lodging expenses. Let me know if you are interested."

I stood there staring at the answering machine, wondering how this was possible. This was, of course, the beginning of my training to become a rebirther. I had read about the founder of rebirthing, Leonard Orr, and his famous student, Sondra Ray, who wrote several books on patterns of thoughts programmed by the person's birth experience. I wanted to meet her, but rumor had it that she was in seclusion and had been so for eight years.

Little did I know this same mysterious hand of fate would schedule our eventual meeting soon.

Chapter 20

Meeting Sondra Ray

One day, a fellow rebirthing practitioner called me to ask if I knew of any books written on the topic of rebirthing. I was surprised she had never heard of Sondra Ray and told her to look her up, and she would find many books on the topic. This particular practitioner was a real go-getter. I knew she would buy, read, and summarize each book in a short time.

I was not expecting her next call. She called breathless with excitement and said, "Thank you for the book recommendations. I scheduled a rebirthing appointment with Sondra Ray. It's next week!" Hold on. "What?" I said, "What? Are you kidding me? She has been in seclusion for over eight years. No one knows where she is." She laughed and said, "Not true. She lives in Marina del Rey. Do you want her phone number?"

Two weeks later, I was driving to Sondra Ray's apartment, thinking this was not real. Her apartment was small but impeccably clean and tastefully decorated with the most exquisite spiritual paintings, statues, and art pieces. She had a special minimally furnished room designated for rebirthing sessions. There was a mat on the floor and an altar with pictures of her guru Babaji along with candles, crystals, and other artifacts.

By this time, I had had several sessions and a rebirthing training with Christina Thomas Fraser. She was clear that the rebirthing process was simple. While the person was breathing, spirit would oversee the release of stuck emotional trauma. She believed only the ego thought it had to get involved with the breathing process. Discussion was done after the session. Rarely, and only if necessary, was there talking during the session. This was my mindset when I arrived for my rebirth session with the famous Sondra Ray.

Her breathing instructions were similar to what I had learned from Christina. She had me lay down and start to breathe. OK, everything seemed on par with what I am used to. Then, the session took an abrupt and unexpected detour. All of a sudden, Sondra tapped my shoulder and said, Babaji wants to talk to you. I will be back. Then she promptly left the room.

I was first surprised, then irritated, then angry. Who leaves a person during a session? What did she mean I needed to talk to Babaji? What kind of bullcrap was this? Did she do this so she could have lunch and come back to charge me for a session she didn't do? I realized none of this negative mental chatter was helping me. I was here. She was a rebirthing icon, and either I trust her or I don't. Either way, I would have to pay for this session, so I might as well trust the process.

My eyes were still closed. I said silently in my head, "Hello?" I was shocked to hear an immediate response that seemed to fill my head. Not one to mince words, he got right to the point. I heard, "As long as you stay up in that safe nest of yours, you will stay stuck. You will never be happy or reach enlightenment from that perch. You need to leap out of that nest in order to fly." I knew intuitively he meant to leave my marriage. I was terrified to do that and was trying to think of anything else I could do instead. And I was determined. I had spent 11 years trying to find a loophole that would allow me to stay married.

Babaji, or whoever this was, continued. "It will be difficult in the beginning, but I will be there to help you through this transition." It was suddenly clear: I realized staying married was not a real option if I truly wanted to be happy and spiritually grow. All of a sudden, I saw a bright white light. I felt so peaceful as I stared at that light and started moving toward it. I felt a bliss overcome my whole body.

The next thing I remember was Sondra was back in the room, shaking me violently, commanding me, "Get back in your body!" I was jolted from that blissful state and was back in the room on the mat. "Why did you do that?" I demanded angrily. She told me that moments before Babaji said, "You better get back in there. She is leaving her body." Sondra said that the light I was so fond of was not a good place to go if I wanted to stay alive. She then stated, "No one dies on my table."

I realized that what she said was true. Just before I saw that bright light, I had the thought that I would rather die than break up my family. It was then I knew how scared I was to be true to myself and do what I needed to do. It would still take me several years to take that leap of faith Babaji was telling me about.

My survival instinct was strong, and I just didn't believe I could survive as a single mom.

I trained with Sondra Ray and discovered how deeply our thinking patterns were programmed at birth. It turns out she was a neonatal nurse before her rebirthing training. She witnessed firsthand the first moments of a baby's birth experience and realized that experience created thought patterns and a blueprint that would impact that baby's entire life.

Her books *Rebirthing In The New Age,* and *Healing And Holiness,* explain how the birth experience sets up a pattern of thinking that has an extensive impact on a person's life. She believed both the birth experience and early childhood programmed a "personal lie" that formed how that person responded to their life experiences. For instance, if you weren't wanted at conception, you might have the personal lie, "I am not wanted."

The Personal Lie In Action

In general, people usually do one of three things with their personal lies.

1. They act it out. If the personal lie is "I am not wanted", they will create situations in which they are not wanted.
2. They will project onto others that their job, mate, body, car, house, and life is not wanted.
3. They will overcompensate to make darn sure they are wanted. This manifests as perfectionistic behavior, working too hard, and worrying about what others think of them.

To put this in perspective, imagine the person with the personal lie, "I am not wanted". If they act it out, they will create social situations, job interviews, and attempts to find a partner in which they are not wanted. In other words, they will feel no one wants to interact with them at parties and will think they won't get the job after the interview. They will think no one wants to have a relationship with them.

If they project it, they will feel perpetually dissatisfied with every aspect of their life and waste years making adjustments and setting goals, not realizing this personal lie is blocking that ever-elusive contentment. No matter how hard the person tries, there will be some detail about their house, their car, their job, their mate, their children, and even their dog or cat that will have something that needs improvement in some way.

If they overcompensate, they will work themselves ragged to ensure excellence in every aspect of their lives, not realizing the underlying fear of not being wanted is what is driving their behavior. I can affirm this was the case in my own life. Despite not wanting to get pregnant until five years after marrying, my mother conceived me during her honeymoon. Because she went from living at home with her parents directly to that honeymoon, you can imagine the great disappointment my sudden and unwanted existence created.

Once you have identified your personal lie, you transform it by affirming your Eternal Truth. This is the opposite of your personal life. Here is a list of personal lies and their opposing eternal truths:

Personal Lie	Eternal Truth
1. I am not wanted.	1. I am wanted.
2. I can't.	2. I can.
3. I am not good enough.	3. I am perfect as I am.
4. I am unlovable.	4. I am love.
5. I am worthless.	5. I am worthy.

Before I learned of this pattern, I would imagine during every social interaction, every party, or other gatherings that I was unwanted and no one liked me or wanted to talk to me. I think my mom's first reaction when she learned she was pregnant was "No!" Then I think when I grew big enough to create movement in her uterus, the thought of me started to shift to curiosity. Then, when I was born, she was in.

My fellow rebirthing friends have told me that because of this pattern, they don't invite me to events too far in advance. They said their experience is that I always say "NO!" and only as the date draws close do I change my response to "YES!" I was amused that my rebirthing friends were able to decode this pattern of behavior about which even I was unaware.

One of my clients was a breech birth, and this caused his mother much pain as his hard skull pressed on her spine during his descent down the birth canal. This programmed him with the belief he hurts women. During his adult life, he lived this pattern by emotionally hurting the women he dated.

And, because in breech births, the baby is often turned upside down and backward, I was astonished at just how many breech birth clients would get lost on their way to my office for their first session and how many late births would be late for their appointments.

I also noticed the cesarean births had specific programming. When the baby could not work their way out of the birth canal without assistance, they would often experience obstacles in their adult lives when trying to meet their goals, or they might think they cannot meet their goals without assistance. Their personal lie was often, "I can't". I had another client whose mother contemplated abortion before he was born. He had the personal lie that the world was not a safe place.

To add to the fun reality of programmed patterning, I found out we often end up with partners whose patterning fits like a hand in a glove with ours. For instance, one partner with the personal lie, "I am bad", may find themselves in a relationship with a partner with the personal lie, "I am unlovable", It may play out like this: The one whose personal lie is "I am bad", might have several affairs during the marriage. The one whose personal lie is, "I am unlovable", will blame their un-lovableness as the cause for those affairs.

I learned during rebirthing training that the purpose of relationships is to heal and transform those negative thought patterns. When the shift happens, the relationship might end, so the partners have an opportunity to heal other patterns with new partners. If partners break up without healing these patterns, they might find they keep having the same relationship with different partners. They might complain, "Why do I keep attracting partners that do...?"

One nuance of projecting personal lies on others, I discovered, was called "shadows". Shadows are unclaimed or rejected parts of ourselves that we push away and that shows up in our lives via other people.

Chapter 21

Shadow Dancing

Throughout my spiritual exploration, I found I was being guided through books. I would go to the metaphysical bookstore and stand in front of a wall of books and wait for one book to jump out at me. I believed some invisible force was guiding me to these books in this manner.

During one bookstore visit, I saw a book that intrigued me: *The Dark Side of the Light Chasers* by Debbie Ford. In this book, she explained in great detail how we project rejected aspects of ourselves onto others. These, she said, were called *Shadows*. She shared how, when we project the parts of ourselves that we don't like, they boomerang back into our lives. For example, one time, when she was speaking in front of a group, a heckler shouted, "You are a bitch!" She was startled at the verbal attack but admitted to herself that she was, in fact, a bitch at times. She hid this by acting über nice all the time.

What she discovered was there was a benefit to her bitchiness she never acknowledged. Her bitchiness got things done. She often championed the rights of the underdogs when they were unable or unwilling to assert themselves. When she embraced rather than pushing away her "bitch" energy, she stopped attracting people who saw her that way.

I shared this information with one of my clients, and she shared a fascinating story that, in my mind, perfectly illustrated how "shadow dancing" worked. She said one day, her daughter, then four years old, accused her of being a terrible mother. On that particular day, she was feeling good about her parenting and felt unfazed by her daughter's judgment.

Frustrated by the lack of response, her daughter then approached her brother, six years old, and said, "You are a murderer." He said, "What? What are you talking about?" She went on to explain that one time when she was three, he pushed her into a toy chest, with her folded over, and wouldn't let her out. She said in that folded position, she couldn't breathe, and she could've died. He snorted. "Well, you didn't die, so I'm not a murderer." She insisted, "But I could've." His response, "Yeah, but you didn't."

My client found her daughter's behavior perplexing. All day she switched between telling her she was a bad mother and declaring her brother a murderer. That night when her husband came home from work, they were seated on the patio. He asked her, "Did I tell you what happened with Julie (their daughter) yesterday?" "No, what happened?"

Her husband then said, "You know that nest the bird built in the backyard" He pointed to the nest in the corner of the patio, lodged in a light fixture. He continued, "Julie kept begging me to let her have one of the baby birds, insisting she would make a good mother. I kept telling her if she took the bird out of the nest, the mother would reject it, and it would die. She went ahead and took one of the baby birds out of the nest and then later put it back. The next morning, I found the baby bird dead on the patio, below the nest."

My client said the explanation about shadows explained her daughter's strange behavior. Her daughter loved animals, so the realization she wasn't a good bird mother and her actions resulted in its death was too much for her to handle. So, she then projected her negative feelings about herself, that she was a bad mother and a murderer to her family. I thought this was a powerful example of shadow.

Little did I know I would experience a powerful example of shadow in my own life. I recall this one rebirthing client. She was a new client in her mid-40s who had meditated a lot in her life. She had never had a rebirthing session before. During her session, she said she traveled to another dimension (not an unusual occurrence during the rebirth sessions). I think this experience was too much for her mind to handle.

After her session, she acted as if she had Alzheimer's. She asked me four or five times if she paid me after she had already paid me. She seemed very disoriented. Another client, who referred her to me, had given her a ride to my office. I told her to take this woman home so she could rest.

I thought this client would be fine after she rested and integrated her rebirthing experience. Then the next day, I got a call from that client's husband. He wanted to know what had happened during her session because she was acting strange, i.e., very disoriented and forgetful. I thought to myself, oh no, this is the end of my practice. I am going to jail. I told him she was ungrounded and to have her drink water and eat vegetables that were grounding like carrots and potatoes. *Yes, I actually gave him this dopey advice because I didn't know what else to do.*

The next day, the husband called again and left a message that after eating many carrots and potatoes, his wife was no different. After listening to that message, I immediately called my friend, Richard Skeie, because I had no idea what to do and felt terrified. He said this was shadow energy at work. He asked me what the one thing was I didn't think I could do as a healer?

After several unsuccessful guesses, I said, "Richard, just tell me. I don't have time for this!" Then he said, "Harm. The one thing you don't think as a healer you could do is harm a client." I thought about that and realized that was true. I definitely did not consider that as a possibility when working with clients, as my intent was to help and heal. As I thought about this, a call-waiting buzz sounded during our call. (Some of you might be too young to remember this phone feature. A buzz would sound when someone was trying to call you while you were talking to someone else.)

I told Richard I would call him back and answered the incoming call. It was the husband again. This time he called to say his wife shifted back to her old self. He said, "She is feeling great. She says everything looks more in focus and the colors around her are brilliant. She is happy, and everything is fine now." I couldn't believe things shifted so fast right when I called back a shadow I didn't even realize was there.

It was during this time of great learning and expansion, Sondra said, "If you really want to advance spiritually, come to India with us and shave your head."

Chapter 22

India: High-Frequency Adventures

Sondra invited me to join her on her annual India trip, where they stay at the Haidakhan ashram during the nine-day Divine Mother Navaratri spring festival.

There were nineteen of us traveling with Sondra to the ashram for Navaratri (the Divine Mother Festival lasting ten days and nine nights). The purpose of Navaratri is to honor the energy aspect of God in the form of the Divine Feminine or Universal Mother. It is believed that God's energy is motionless, and the Divine Mother energy gives that motionless energy a form in life. The Divine Mother is referred to as "Durga", which literally means "the remover of the miseries of life".

The nine-day festival is divided into three sets of three days. The first three days, Durga is invoked to remove all of our impurities. For the next three days, Durga is worshipped as the giver of spiritual wealth. During the final set of three days, Durga is worshipped as the giver of wisdom. It is believed we need the blessings of these three aspects of Durga or Divine Mother (purity, abundance, and wisdom) for all-around success in life.[18]

One thing I would notice right away was the strange way this trip would invoke our greatest lessons. For instance, one of the trip participants was an image consultant. She had packed her necessary makeup and wardrobe very carefully to look her best during the trip. She was the only one whose luggage was lost during transit and was not recovered for the duration of the trip.

It appeared as if whatever fear or issue you had played out in some form during this trip. I discover that India, and the ashram more so, has such a high frequency that thoughts materialize much faster. Sondra makes this trip yearly to gradually and continually increase her vibration. I think it is working, as she radiates an intense frequency that is palpable in her presence. This trip, more than any other in my life, would bring up lessons and issues I was not even aware needed addressing.

In general, I don't enjoy traveling. I am a bit of a homebody. But I *am* a sucker for working vacations, where you get something accomplished in an amazing, scenic location. When she said the energy is so high in India that you get thirteen years of spiritual evolution for each of the nine festival days, I couldn't resist making the trip.

She had also mentioned that many people shave their heads by the Ganges River during the festival as a spiritual purification, and she said if you kept your head shaved for nine months (like a pregnancy), you were reborn (spiritually). *I look back on this time, and I don't know what was in my head to agree to all this. I must have been desperate to be someone else: someone else who was spiritual and pure.*

It's Britney @#!!

During this time, my husband and I had been separated for over a year but were still on somewhat friendly terms. I was living in an apartment, and the children would live with me for two weeks, then switch to their dad's for two weeks. The week I was scheduled to leave for India, pop-star Britney Spears shaved her head and made news headlines.

Head shaving was not well known at this time. This was the first time head-shaving became a public phenomenon. My husband called me to inform me he planned to tell all our friends that the reason I shaved my head was to be like Britney Spears. Awesome.

You Are Uninvited

As I prepared for this trip, I asked a lot of questions. What do you eat? I was told you only ate once a day at noon, and it would be a simple vegetarian meal. I was told the bathrooms were holes in the floor, and you needed to squat. I was told to be sure not to drink the water, or I would get a bad case of diarrhea.

There were no lights or running electricity. Bring a headlamp, they advised, as you needed to walk down the mountain each morning at four a.m. and wash in the Ganges river before the first chanting session at five a.m. If you did not first clean yourself in this fashion, you could not enter the temple, as you were considered dirty. If you had your period, you could also not enter the temple. Also, there were no bathrooms to shower in, except the river Ganges.

Sondra advised that no one could wear regular street clothing. To respect and honor the ashram culture and tradition, we needed to dress at all times in the traditional Indian sari dress and pants with the sash.

None of this sounded terrible or that difficult, but honestly, the eating once a day, the showering in the Ganges at four a.m. in front of everyone, and the constant threat of diarrhea with only a few toilet areas serving the entire ashram sounded scary. I silently worried about this but did not mention my concerns to my travel partner and friend, Kevin.

I met Kevin at one of Sondra's rebirthing trainings shortly after that first session when Babaji had instructed me to jump out of the nest. He and I became friends and, during that training, I asked him what he did for a living before he retired from 24 years in the Air Force. His answer: I was a jump instructor. *I can't make this stuff up. We have remained good friends until this day.*

The day before our departure, Kevin called the airline to confirm our flight was still scheduled. The attendant informed Kevin that our flight was canceled, which was weird because we hadn't received any notifications. She told him to hold, and she would check to see when the flight was rescheduled. This was a problem. Our flight was timed exactly to meet the rest of the group in Delhi. From there were bus departures to little neighboring towns and then a long jeep ride up the mountain to the ashram.

This was not a journey that could be replicated on our own. Sondra had many connections in India and had made this trip for many years. So if our flight was canceled, the whole trip was in jeopardy. Kevin was on hold for an hour and a half while I kept packing just in case we were still leaving.

Then he asked me to stay on the phone, so he could finish packing. I agreed and held the phone to my ear (cell phones were not a thing at this time, so it was a regular plug-in wall phone). As I waited for the woman to come back on the line, I had the distinct feeling I had been uninvited to Babaji's ashram because of all my fears and worries. I cannot tell you why I had that feeling, just that the feeling was very strong.

I felt ashamed and embarrassed that I was being such a baby and that I was not honoring the chance to visit this sacred ashram. I had only been on the phone for about five minutes, but I knew I needed to do something. I never had silent conversations with Babaji, but I did that day. I silently apologized for not appreciating the great opportunity to visit his ashram (he was not alive at this time and had transitioned in 1984). I said I would trust any decision he made, and if he was uninviting me, I would accept that and, in the future, not take this opportunity for granted.

I had just finished that silent prayer when the woman immediately came back on the phone and said, "Your flight is back on." I asked, "What? Why? How is that possible?" She repeated, "Your flight is back on," and promptly hung up the phone. That is the moment I knew this was going to be a wild ride.

The plane ride was uneventful. It was as if there had been no cancellation at all. When we arrived in India, the one thing I noticed right away was that the sky was brown and not blue. There seemed to be a haze coating the whole area (I was told this was due to the country's practice of burning trash). I was instantly grateful for the Environmental Protection Agency (EPA) in my country.

There were also monkeys running loose everywhere. No one seemed to think this was unusual. Sondra had arranged for us to stay a couple of nights in Delhi (to get us used to the transition to the ashram, which had none of the comforts of city life).

The Head Shave

For some reason, I was never hesitant about getting my head shaved. I don't know why because hair has always been my thing. I was excited to do it and couldn't wait. The barber was in his 90s and apparently used to shave Babaji's head right there at the Ganges River when he was alive. There were about twenty of us in Sondra's group, and about half of us were getting our heads shaved on the designated head-shaving day.

When it was my turn, I knelt before the barber (who spoke no English). He motioned for me to bow my head, and he began dry shaving my head with a very dull stick shaver. I wondered if this was the same shaver he used on Babaji because I thought he was going to scalp me with every loud scrape across my head. Each of us was assigned a partner to support us during our head shaves, and Kevin was my support partner.

When he finished, the barber tilted my head up, looked into my eyes, and said, "You remind me of Babaji" (in perfectly clear English). I stared back at him and said nothing. I had heard of things called *leelas* that happened here. Leelas were little dramas that happened to teach people about their egos and fears. I thought this must be a leela because telling me I reminded him of Babaji was definitely a head trip. I said nothing to Kevin or the group about this, and no one said anything to me about it.

At the time of the head shavings, our group sat on these large cement stairs and sang chants to lend their support. Some of the group were on the top of the stairs, far from us, with a view of the river. After my head was shaved, I felt a huge wave of burning hot energy pouring through the top of my head. It was almost unbearable. I could also hear people's thoughts, which was also unbearable. But none of this was as upsetting as when I looked at me for the first time, post head shave.

For most of my life, I had hated my eyebrows which, to me, looked like two thick jet-black caterpillars above my eyes. Even after I learned to pluck them, they were still pretty thick and unwieldy. I had always kept bangs to hide them, which I forgot about until my head was bald. Now those eyebrows were on broad display. I looked like the offspring of Groucho Marx and Mr. Clean. I felt nakedly ugly and exposed. There was literally nothing I could do to remedy this. I decided I would buy one of the beautiful scarves at the ashram gift shop, but the ashram obviously didn't care about sales because every time I visited there, it was closed.

Your Name Is Mala

One of the perks of being in India with Sondra Ray was her connection to the head of the ashram, Muniraj. He was the successor to Babaji, and getting a private meeting with him was rare. Because Sondra had known Babaji personally and had been going to the ashram for over 30 years, she was able to arrange private meetings with Muniraj for each group she took to India.

It was during this private meeting he would look into your eyes and give you your very own spiritual name. He was supposedly giving you the name that reflected your true spiritual essence. It was a big deal, and everyone was excited about this part of the trip.

The day before our private meeting, we were scheduled to go in groups to visit the cave in which Babaji was rumored to have materialized back in 1970. The energy was supposedly so intense in there that you could only go in for about ten or fifteen minutes. Sondra had organized small groups of four to five people going in every thirty minutes during a two-hour period. She emphasized that it was important to be at the cave at the designated time, or it would throw off the entire schedule.

That day, the gift shop was finally open when I ventured over there. The line was long but moving fairly quickly. I found the perfect scarf and was happy I finally had something to cover my bald head. When I was finally only a couple of customers away from the cashier, the line suddenly stopped moving. It remained immobile for several minutes, and now it was getting close to the time I needed to head over to the cave. I kept glancing at my watch, telling myself there was plenty of time. I knew I should leave, but I kept rationalizing that I would make it in time.

Truth be told, I made the decision I was going to get that scarf, cave be damned. I knew this was a test, and I also knew I was flunking. When I arrived at the cave, my group was furious and would not speak to me. We had been bumped and had to wait thirty minutes to go into the cave. I didn't dare show or tell anyone about the scarf.

I don't remember much about the cave, except that I was relieved I wasn't struck down by lightning or something when I entered. The consequences of my actions came full force the next day.

The next day was the meeting with Muniraj when we received our spiritual names. Everyone wanted awesome names like Goddess of the Light or Healer of Light. The woman before me was named Goddess of something or another; I can't remember, only that the word Goddess was in there. I watched Muniraj and marveled at how calm and stern he looked. But, I felt like he scowled at me as I knelt before him.

He stared at me for what seemed like a long time, eyes boring into me. Then he took a breath and delivered my new name. "Your name is Mala," he said. Excuse me? My name is Mala? Not Goddess of the Light? It wasn't even the name of a living thing: it was an object, the necklace that adorned the Divine Mother statue and was also used to count chants for meditation.

In other words, I was an inanimate object used to adorn statues. The irony and the meaning felt really clear to me, and my face reddened in embarrassment at this realization. Before, the only thing that mattered to me was to adorn my head rather than to respect the time agreement I had made to Sondra and my group.

I felt ashamed and really bummed that my true priorities were memorialized in my new spiritual name. A hard lesson for sure.

Message From Babaji

After my head was shaved, I walked to the main dining area for lunch. As I walked by, I noticed that many of the older Indian men in the ashram looked intently at me. I thought to myself, this is also part of the leela, and I am not falling for it. The next day, one of the women in our group approached Kevin and me. She asked, "What did Babaji say to you when he finished your head shave?" I said, "Oh, I don't know."

Now, she was one of the people that sat way up high, far removed from the river's edge, so I was surprised when she said, "I heard him say 'You remind me of Babaji' in perfect English, but he doesn't speak English." Kevin then said, "I heard that too." I turned to Kevin and asked, "Why didn't you say anything about that?" He said, "You didn't say anything about it, so I thought I imagined it since he doesn't speak English." The woman asked, "What do you think it means?" I said, "Probably nothing." And we left it at that.

A couple of days later, I was peeling potatoes with the other ashram volunteers, helping with the noon meal preparations. Another woman from our group approached me. She announced, "I have a message from Babaji." A few of the women claimed to channel messages from Babaji, and she was one of them. Truth be told, I wasn't sure I believed in these messages.

I was prepared for some airy-fairy mumbo jumbo message. I just stared at her waiting for the message. She continued, "He said I look like you. Is that so bad?" I asked, "That's the whole message?" She nodded and left. I sat there pondering the meaning of this strange message. Then as the meaning of this message hit me, tears ran down my face. I realized why the barber said I reminded him of Babaji (I wondered if that message came from Babaji himself, who was known to speak in Hindi, but people would hear the message in their native language). I also understood why the men in the ashram kept staring at me. I realized with my shaved head, dark brown eyes, and thick black eyebrows, I looked like a young Babaji with his head shaved.

All of a sudden, my self-image issues seemed to melt away. I felt comfortable with my eyebrows and the way I looked for perhaps the first time in my life. It was a true healing for me.

Payback Is A @#!

About three days after our arrival at the ashram, my right shoulder started hurting so much that I had to hold it up with my left arm. The weight of it hanging caused too much pain. I wasn't sure why this pain was occurring, but there was nothing I could do about it, so I just endured it.

One day, Sondra told me she had arranged for me to do a healing trade with the acupuncturist from Japan who worked on Muniraj and many of the ashram visitors. I felt honored to work on him. He did not speak English, so a translator was present during our mutual session. I told him I would work on him first since he was so tired and his body was in pain from working so much during the festival.

I worked on his hips, back, and shoulders. I could feel his body relaxing, and soon, he was fast asleep.

I whispered to the translator not to wake him up and that he didn't need to work on me. He seemed so tired I didn't want to wake him just so he could work on me.

When I returned to our area in the ashram and told Sondra about our session, she said, "Oh no, he was supposed to work on you and heal your arm! Now, what are we going to do?" I did not know why he was supposed to work on my arm, and now I was freaked out, thinking I was going to have this intense arm pain for good.

Each day in the afternoon, Sondra would have us do a group rebirth session on the large balcony outside our sleeping quarters. On this day, as I lay getting ready to breathe, Sondra knelt down and whispered as she walked by, "Breathe on the life when your arm was injured. We have to get to the bottom of this to heal it." I had not often had rebirth sessions when I saw visions from past lives, but India was a different place, so I thought anything was possible.

As my breathing became rhythmic, I started to see a scene before me. In it, I saw the acupuncturist, but he was a young boy dressed as a ninja, and I was also a male, older than the acupuncturist. We were running on a grassy mountainside together. It was obvious the acupuncturist looked up to me like an older brother figure. We both had swords. Sondra was our leader (also a male) in this lifetime. I was her second in command and was envious of her power. I wanted to be the one in charge. I beheaded her, but as soon as I did so, I realized that she had been lifting me up with her power, and with her gone, all the power drained from me as well.

The acupuncturist was horrified by my actions. He loved me but was loyal to Sondra and swiftly sliced off my right arm, the arm that had performed that deadly deed. As I watched this scene unfold, I realized that all the players from that life were reunited here in India. So Sondra was right; the acupuncturist was supposed to work on me to make up for the amputation he had done on me in that lifetime. I guess witnessing this past life shifted the energy because the next day, the pain was gone.

This experience felt like my imagination. It was so hard to know what to believe out there.

Excuse Me Miss, But Your Head Is Exploding

One requirement Sondra had for India attendees was prior rebirthing sessions. She believed the energy was so high in India, and she didn't have the time or energy to babysit people who had not released some of their emotional trauma before experiencing the intense energies at the ashram. On this trip, she made an exception for one woman who had admitted anger issues and no prior rebirthing experiences.

It turned out this was probably not a good idea. If I had not witnessed this with my own eyes, I would not have believed it. This woman must have felt a lot of anger and was suppressing it while at the ashram. The anger energy had nowhere to go, so it expanded her head. Her head blew up to twice its normal size, and her eyes were swollen shut. She was seen by the ashram doctors, but no one could figure out what was wrong with her. She remained in that state until the day before we were scheduled to leave, and then her head unexplainably returned to its normal size.

Doggie Patrol

On the last night of the trip, five of us in the group wanted to visit Babaji's cave before we left. We were all excited and a bit nervous because it was dark and there was no one around as far as the eyes could see. We traveled down the 108 steps down to the river's edge, getting ready to cross the small bridge to the cave sight. As we approached the bridge, all of a sudden, this dog appeared out of nowhere and grabbed Kevin's pants with its teeth and pulled as if to prevent him from moving forward.

We laughed and shrugged this off as the antics of a playful pup. Then he grabbed the skirt of one of the women and also pulled her back as if to say, "You cannot go any further." After that, Kevin said, "Ok, that's it, I'm not going." It was then that one of the women in the group said, "I'm sorry." We all turned to her and waited for her to explain. She then said a little sheepishly, "I 'm on my period." We all let out a collective gasp. That was forbidden. We realized this was why the dog wouldn't let us proceed. We looked for him, but he had vanished. There was a huge expanse of open area but no sign of the dog at all.

Chapter 23

Remote Possibilities

When I returned from India, I worried how my new hairstyle (or lack of it) would be received in the community. I had already been given a wide berth from the weird energy healing practice, then getting divorced, and now donning a shiny bald head. I imagined people really did think I was emulating Britney Spears. The thing is, I really didn't care. People could think of me as the strangest person on earth, but I was trying to attain something they might not consider worth attaining: inner wealth vs. outer wealth, i.e., inner worth vs. outer worth.

I'd like to say that this aspiration was grounded and balanced, but as I have heard many times, the ego is a shapeshifter. And what that means is the ego will transform into anything you think, say, or do and make it about Itself. If you are charitable, the ego will inflate your sense of worthiness for your generosity. If you have decided money is not the ultimate goal and you have donned a loincloth and begging bowl, your ego will pat you on the back for it and make you feel special.

There it is again, that need to feel special. I knew this was a trick of the ego, but I still hadn't seen through this illusion yet. It still felt good to be just a little different than everyone in my immediate circle. Whereas before I felt scared to be different, now I reveled in it. This would be a self-built pedestal from which I would tumble. For now, I was feeling special and loving it.

The India trip only added to my inflated sense of self. But behind all those feelings of self-importance was something else brewing under the surface. What I did not realize at the time was I was collecting information and modalities because I had the false assumption that, with enough energy tools in my toolbox, I could control my life. And by life, I meant my health, wealth, and joy.

Don't get me wrong, I had a lot of impressive tools in that box. I just didn't realize those tools, while powerful, had limitations.

At this time, though, I was still chasing that energetic high and marveling at the miracles around me. It was at this time that I discovered healing could be done remotely. I attended a lecture with a friend and fellow energy healer, Dr. Robert Jeffrey.[19] That night, I was on the brink of getting really sick and had the accompanying chills, headache, cough, extreme fatigue, and runny nose. I was so sick I was appalled at my inconsiderate decision to attend this lecture. Dr. Jeffrey understood with no judgment.

The next morning I woke up with no symptoms. My energy was back; I had no headache, chills, cough, or runny nose. In fact, I felt completely well. Dr. Jeffrey called me at 11 a.m. and asked how I was feeling. I told him I felt completely well, and he said, "Cool." I asked why that was cool and why he was calling. He explained he had done remote healing on my flu symptoms the night before when he arrived home.

I asked him what modality he used, and he said, "The NeuroModulation Technique." I thought I was progressive, believing in energy healing, but I had never heard of or experienced remote healing. Nor had I experienced so fast a healing with infectious agents. I signed up for the training the following week.

Flash forward several years, and I received a call from a young client who was about to board a plane and was experiencing intense ear pain. She had caught a virus that had overtaken her during a short trip visiting friends in another state. She was afraid she would burst an eardrum if she boarded the plane. She must have felt desperate because, at that time, I did not offer my clients remote healings.

I did them for my children. By now, my soon-to-be ex-husband and I were living permanently apart, and the children were living with each of us part-time. When they were with their dad, I worked on my son Tei, who was in travel ball and always injured in some way or another, remotely. It worked, and the children would often call me for remote healings. *Tei, now 27, still calls for those remote healings.*

This client said I didn't tell her I could do remote healings, and she just hoped there was something I could do as she was about to board her plane. After I texted her that her treatment had been done, she reported back that her ear pain had lessened quickly, and she was able to board the plane and fly home without incident.

My mind was still unsure how this remote killing of bacteria was possible when I came across a YouTube video in which Dr. Royal Rife films paramecium swimming around on a microscopic slide. (Dr. Rife was an American inventor and scientist, best known in the 1930s for subjecting diseased body cells to harmful frequencies that would kill them).[20] He then directs an energy frequency towards the paramecium, and you can see the live paramecium go from being alive and swimming around to suddenly imploding and liquifying in real-time.

This video explained to me that when we direct energy, it can and does effect change in other matter, even remotely. *It would take many more years, however, for my clients to accept and trust remote healings. It was not until the pandemic in 2020 that clients, out of desperation, started booking remote sessions.*

I would then discover that healings, whether remote or in-person, are exponentially strengthened when you love the recipient. This would be proven to me time and again over the years. I can only assume love, which has a higher frequency, packs a stronger healing punch.

I remember the time my mother had a heart attack and required triple bypass surgery. (I do not think it is a coincidence that her best friend (my dad) of 45 years had died a couple of years before, and she was literally and figuratively heartbroken over this tragic and unexpected loss). My mother's surgery was completed at 6 p.m., and the hospital staff advised me to go home and rest as she would be unconscious and heavily sedated for the rest of the night.

As I slept in blissful ignorance, my mother bled nonstop for the next 11 hours, according to the doctors.

At 5 a.m., my mother's attending nurse called to inform me of this ongoing and urgent post-surgery development. The nurse asked me to come to the hospital as soon as possible. It was now 5:15 a.m. As I was getting dressed, my mother's fire alarm went off. But here is the weird thing; There was no fire, and this alarm was not the usual loud, annoying beep. Instead, it was a female voice yelling, "Fire! Fire! Fire!" *A couple of years later, I asked my mom what happened to the other alarm with the female voice yelling fire. She said, "What? I have never had a fire alarm that did that!"*

I was immediately aware of my father's presence and his urgent nudging to do something to help my mother. The only tissue-repair healing technique I knew could be done quickly and remotely was the NeuroModulation Technique. This work was done by reading very specific energy healing instructions to the body. And, if you do not understand what you are reading, the treatment has no effect. *This is probably why my results were inconsistent. It took me several years to understand the written protocols, but fortunately, the tissue repair protocol was one of the ones I did understand.*

I pulled out my manual and started reading aloud. Ten minutes later, I was done. I immediately called the hospital, and after 11 hours of nonstop bleeding, the nurse said the bleeding had suddenly stopped. It had only been 30 minutes since their first call.

During this same time period, my friend Kevin was scheduled to undergo a heart valve replacement surgery to correct a congenital heart valve defect. The admitting nurse, on doctor's orders, gave him a dose of blood pressure medicine, which plummeted his already low heart rate. As a life-saving mechanism, his body responded by shutting down his liver and kidneys.

Now the doctors could not perform the surgery but, if they didn't, he could die. For three days, I watched the doctors and nurses running around frantically doing tests, giving him medications intravenously, and showing signs that they were doing everything they could to get his kidneys and liver functioning again so he could withstand the surgery.

Then, on the fourth day, I noticed a marked change. My friend's hospital room was suddenly a ghost town. No doctors or nurses were coming to his room, and I had a bad feeling in the pit of my stomach. At midnight, I asked the night nurse to be straight with me. His response shocked me. He said, "Honestly, your friend is dying. You best get everyone here as soon as possible to say their goodbyes."

With nothing to lose, I rushed home and did the NeuroModulation Technique remotely. I instructed the healing to repeat itself indefinitely. It was 2 a.m. when I finished. The next morning I arrived at the hospital to find Kevin's hospital bed empty. I panicked, fearing he had died during the night, and quickly contacted the nurse. She informed me that early that morning, his liver and kidney suddenly started working, and he was transferred from the Intensive Care Unit to the Intermediate Care Unit. He had recovered enough to withstand the heart valve transplant and is alive and well today.

Before you frantically search for my contact information to schedule a healing, know that this was an unusual incident. I am not able to do this on command whenever I want. This system works sometimes, and other times it does not. This work is so inconsistent (when I do it) that I only do this with friends and family and no longer offer it as part of my practice.

I include these stories because they had an effect on what I believed was possible. My ego, ever shape-shifting and making its presence known, was convinced these occurrences were not random, but with the right training and focus, could be manifested more consistently. I think this is the loop addicts travel within. For drug addicts, they chase that first astounding high, thinking this next hit will replicate that first amazing high. For gambling addicts, they convince themselves that this next bet will give them the big payoff.

It's the inconsistent but existent successes that can keep a person hoping and trying to duplicate. As I learned even more amazing things about our miraculous Universe, this hope just grew.

Chapter 24

Quantum Living

These experiences did not occur in a time cluster. I share them in this chapter because they fall within a single category, which I've termed "destroying thoughts and beliefs that were previously in place". These were incidents that I could neither explain nor deny. During this time, I still held fast to the hope that if enough of these strange occurrences could be strung together or repeated, I would either gain control of my life or become enlightened. Either or both were on the table of possibilities, and this became my *raison d'etre*.

Alternate Realities

We were taking a break from a QEST continuing education weekend when the instructor, Judith Heath,[21] usually not inclined to tell "woo woo" stories, shared a strange thing that had been happening with her clients over the prior two months. First, she was having dreams about the work being done in Egypt. She saw a stone structure with earthen walls. The doorway in the east wall had an opening with a short wall behind it (like in airport bathrooms). The work was being done in that room, with the clients lying on stone slab tables.

She shared how recently two clients suddenly sat up during their sessions, declaring that there were tall beings in the room. One of the two clients, a male, said the beings said this work had been done in Egypt. Two other clients also randomly mentioned, unprompted, that the work had originated in Egypt. These client declarations corroborated the dreams Judith had about the work being done in Egypt.

We were trying to take in this strange story when another QEST teacher, Paula Martin Burns,[22] shared her story about QEST's possible origins. The weekend Princess Diana died in 1977, Paula attended an open mic gathering featuring a channeled entity called 'Bashar.' A microphone was passed around, and each person could ask a question. Paula prefaced her question by saying she had learned a modality, using a numerical language that vibrationally communicated with the human body. She asked Bashar from where did this modality originate.

Bashar told her it originated in Atlantis, came through Egypt, and into the United States. He told her if one understood mathematics and sacred geometry, the templates of the body could be put together.

I asked Paula, "Why did you wait eight years to share this story, and did you find out the missing sacred geometry?" Paula shrugged and laughed, saying, "I don't know, and no, I am not good with math." Not good with math? Are you kidding me?

After that class, I was on the hunt for anything that taught more about sacred geometry. I knew little

1991

about the subject. I found out sacred geometry ascribes symbolic and sacred meanings to certain geometric shapes and in certain geometric proportions. Sacred geometry is an ancient science, the information of which could fill several books.

One sacred geometric pattern I discovered was called the Flower of Life. The Flower of Life is a geometrical symbol that consists of 19 overlapping circles evenly spaced and interconnected. These overlapping circles form a flower-like pattern within the flower. It is believed to be over 6,000 years old and thought to contain vital information about the secrets and origins of the universe and all living things.

The repeating patterns found in the Flower of Life can be found in many life forms. Some examples are the spirals and petal counts in flowers, the spirals within a sea shell, trees, cloud forms, even the very structure of molecules at the atomic level.[23]

So, when I found a Flower of Life meditation class, I quickly registered. This was the class where I met my friend Archna. She would become a treasured friend and companion for the coming years of metaphysical growth and exploration.

During this workshop, I thought there was something wrong with my eyes. When I stared at the teacher, my eyes would go out of focus, and everyone in the room would disappear, replaced with an opaque white cloud, with only the teacher visible. Only it wouldn't be him. He kept transforming into an old Asian male with a robe and goatee. I needed to know if I was going nuts so, during one of the class breaks, I told the instructor what I was experiencing and asked if he had ever heard that before. He responded that many students had seen him transform into that old Asian man, but he did not know what they saw or why he was showing up that way.

After the break, he asked the class if anyone else was seeing him as an old Asian male and a couple of hands went up. He said we were ready then to hear about alternate realities. He explained it this way. Without fanfare or drama, he said there were alternate realities in which we bounced in and out of all the time. He said we don't jump into realities that are totally different, like being a nurse in one reality and a fireman in another. Rather, we tend to stick to about ten realities that are pretty similar with slight variations. In one reality, we may have a digital alarm clock, and in another, we have a wind-up alarm clock. As we awaken in the new reality, we may have the thought, "Hey, I don't own a digital alarm clock," but as we become more awake and conscious, we adjust to that new reality and think, "Oh yes, I do own a digital alarm clock."

He explained that this was the reason we lose things that we know were in a certain place. They aren't where we left them, and then they reappear in that expected place again. He said we rationalize to ourselves, thinking we just didn't see the object even though it was there. He went on to explain that it is as if we are in the center of a slide carousel, with each slide representing a different reality. (For those of you too young to know this reference, Google it.) He said we slide in and out of these neighboring realities all the time and don't realize it.

He then predicted that now that we had learned of this phenomenon, we would experience it within the next couple of weeks and know what was happening. I was fascinated but not convinced.

The following week, I was attending a healing seminar at a San Diego hotel. In a large conference room, 50 massage tables were set up for the attendees to practice healing on each other. I was paired with a man and worked on him first for ten minutes. Then when it was my turn, I took off my purple Land's End fleece jacket and placed it underneath the massage table. There was nothing else under the massage table and no one standing near us. When the practice session was done, I felt cold and jumped off the table to grab my purple jacket, only to discover there was nothing under the table!

I asked my partner if he had moved my jacket. He glanced under the table, saw nothing, and said, "No, why would I move your jacket?" At this point, I started looking around the room, thinking to myself, "Who would be rude enough to borrow my jacket?" I started alternating between looking under the table and looking around the room, growing more annoyed by the second. On the fifth look under the table, there it was. No one had come near my table, and now there it was exactly how I left it. I realized this was the moment the meditation instructor was talking about. If he hadn't explained this phenomenon, I very well would have explained it away in my mind.

Several years later, it was Christmas, and my daughter was now a teenager. She, my mom, and I were in my bedroom, and my mom asked Haley to sing one of her church choir songs. Haley left my bedroom to retrieve the lyric sheets and returned in about a minute. As she stood at my bedroom door, she pointed to her black cell phone sitting in the middle of my white comforter and said, "Hey, I took my cell phone with me when I left this room. Why is it now on your bed?"

Not amused, I said, "Well, you obviously are mistaken. Just come in and sing the song." But my mom interjected, "Actually, I saw her cell phone in her hand as she left the room." Not letting me dismiss her perceptions, my daughter continued, "Yes, and when I was in my bedroom, I knew I was going to sing for you both, so I fixed my hair in the mirror, and I just saw my cell phone in my hand in the mirror, seconds before I arrived in your bedroom." I took a deep breath and told them, "The fact that you both experienced this together means you are both ready to learn about alternate realities." I explained what I knew, and I expected them both to call me crazy, but they thought that was the only explanation that made sense in light of what they had just experienced.

Each time this happens, my mind wants to make sense of the incongruity. Recently, I was watching television, and when I reached for the remote, it wasn't there. I got off the couch, looked under and around it, but the remote wasn't anywhere. I was tired, so I just unplugged the television and decided I would look for it more carefully the next day.

The next evening, I still could not find the remote, so I took a remote from another room and plugged in the television. But the television would not boot up Netflix, Hulu, or any of the paid streaming channels I had subscribed to. I thought the Roku stick might have become loose, so I looked at the back of the television, and there was no Roku stick! There was no one else in the house at this time, and that Roku stick is hard to pull out of the television. Also, I could not have watched television the night before without it!

I share these stories so you, too, may realize you are jumping in between realities when this happens to you. And speaking of jumping, if you believe the next two stories, then you know teleportation is real.

Teleportation

For those of you who have never heard of teleportation, it's a mode of instantaneous movement in which matter is dematerialized in one location and recreated in another. In other words, you disappear in one location and instantly reappear in another. In my metaphysical research, I read about teleportation and wondered if it was really possible.

One time, a friend of mine, who ran the Babaji ashram in Colorado, and who was visiting Los Angeles, offered to do an event at The Centre. This was a close friend of Sondra Ray. I met her when Sondra took us to stay at the Babaji ashram in Colorado after an advanced rebirthing training. She said she would do anything I asked for the event: chanting, meditation, storytelling about experiences with Babaji when he was alive. She had lived with Babaji for a month at the Babaji ashram in India.

I had never heard any of her Babaji stories. She had never shared her stories before because she believed keeping them secret would maintain their sacredness. Because many Babaji devotees know story sharing is quite rare, this event was very popular. On the night of the event, the room was packed with Babaji devotees hungry for any details about Babaji's life.

Although she shared many stories, there was one story that astounded me. She said Babaji was understandably always surrounded by an entourage of people at the ashram, but one day, she was standing alone staring out at a neighboring mountain. He was alone and held out his hand as if to ask her to put her hand in his.

As soon as she placed her hand in his, she felt and heard a loud whooshing sound, and then both of them were now located atop that mountain that was just seconds ago, part of the distant horizon. She gasped, thinking she was dreaming. He laughed and said, "It's as easy as this." She said to this day that she still wonders if that really happened.

Coincidently, the following week, another instructor was visiting The Centre. We were discussing what talk he might give. Because he had been a NASA engineer for 35 years, I loved to ask him questions about quantum physics and what he knew about time, space, and things like teleportation. I did not tell him about my friend's Babaji story, but I did ask him if he thought teleportation was possible.

He said as a young child, he always believed it was possible. He said his fascination with quantum physics was what prompted him to become a NASA engineer. So convinced was he of its possibility that he had spent his whole life trying to make it happen. He said he would try to imagine he was in another location instantly, but nothing ever happened.

That is, he said, until this one time he was walking with his fellow engineers on the NASA base, and they were walking from one building to another. The other engineers were quite far from him, he estimated, at least half the length of a football field. He imagined, as he always did that, he would disappear and reappear right next to them. He said, "This time, I heard and felt a loud whooshing sound and felt sucked into a tunnel of sorts. Then, instantly, I was next to the other engineers who, just seconds ago, were far in front of me." They were all startled when he was suddenly next to them and said, "Oh, there you are." They did not realize what had happened, and he did not tell them.

He said, "I was afraid to tell anyone about this because I assumed they would think me crazy." In fact, he had just told his wife about this two years before. I was amazed that his story matched my friend's story, so I told him that story. His eyes were wide in wonder when I finished. He said, "Isn't it interesting that she felt and heard that same whooshing sound?" I nodded. He was so grateful because, truthfully, he still thought that occurrence was his imagination. Now he knew in his heart that it was real.

I was realizing that matter contained within time and space was not as locked in as I thought. Time, space, and matter were malleable.

Time Shifting: Or The Joker Wins

In Christina Thomas Fraser's book, *Secrets*,[24] she shared a time-shifting technique that she gave me permission to repeat here. She explained that time was not static but could speed up or slow down, depending on your energy frequency. This made sense to me when I thought of how time flies when I am having fun and slows when I am not. I remember Haley named one of her really boring teachers, "the one who makes time stand still."

Christina said to imagine a clock with the current time, and then imagine arriving at your destination, and imagine the clock with the exact time you want to arrive at that location. She said to add as much detail as I could. For instance, imagine what the air smells like, the sounds you hear, what you see, and how you feel when you arrive.

I had the occasion to test this technique one day when Tei, Haley, and I were late and rushing to his baseball practice, generally a 45-minute drive, without traffic. This day, a Friday at 5:40 p.m., the 6 p.m. start of practice seemed impossible. The freeway traffic looked like a sea of red brake lights, and every lane was stopped. Tei was frustrated with me. "Mom," he whined, "we are going to be late!" (Being late meant no playtime during the weekend games, a punishment worse than death when you are ten).

"I'm sorry, Tei, but there is nothing we can do." Then I remembered the time-shifting technique from Christina's book. I thought it couldn't hurt to try it. But I thought I would elicit help from the kids. We needed all the energy we could get.

I explained how to picture us pulling into the parking lot at 6 p.m. and to imagine the sounds, sights, smells, and even how we would feel arriving on time. They understood and started to imagine our targeted arrival time of 6 p.m.

We were in the fast lane, but the traffic was not moving. Suddenly, just the lane we were in was empty. I cannot explain to you how this was possible, but Tei said, "Go! Mom, Go!" I accelerated but felt really nervous. The lane to our immediate right was at a standstill, and with us going 65 miles an hour, if a car pulled in our lane, the collision would be catastrophic. I kept tapping on my brake, but no one seemed to be moving from that other lane, so I just gunned the gas and went for it.

I do not know why no one was in our lane. It made absolutely no sense. When we took our exit in Monterey Park, the time was five minutes to 6 p.m., but the park was just a couple of blocks away. We would easily make it in time to meet the 6 p.m. deadline.

But then a strange thing happened. I kept getting caught with the red lights, which delayed our progress. By the time we arrived at the park, it was 6:05 p.m. I turned to Tei and Haley as I parked and said, "I don't know what happened. We were on time." Tei giggled from the back seat, saying, "Haha, I imagined 6:05 p.m."

His jokester nature was stronger than his desire to arrive on time, and he probably figured it was close enough to satisfy the coach. I was still trying to figure out how all this was possible and why the Universe listened to Tei's instructions instead of Haley's and my combined directions.

Then I realized something. Tei's jokester energy had a higher frequency than my fear-based energy. With all things being equal, the joker will always win. Fascinating.

Setting an intent was strongly affected by the attitude with which you did it. If you felt attached to healing results, feared that you wouldn't get your desired results, or felt depressed or angry, the energy frequency was not as strong.

The Universe Is Listening, and The Answer Is Yes

In the midst of my explorations, I made what I believed was a revolutionary discovery. In an effort to create continuity and congruence, the Universe reflects back to us the reality we project out. Meaning the reality in which you believe is the reality that you get.

There seems to be a mirroring effect when we have thoughts that take on the energy of *knowing*. If you *know*, not just believe, the Universe to create continuity, then reflects that reality back to you. I believe that is why most manifestation instructions advise you to imagine you already have what you want. When you do so, the Universe reflects that reality back to you.

I realized that this could affect you in little-known ways that you may not intend. For instance, if you keep wishing you had another car or job, you are telling the Universe you don't have that particular car or job. You will be stuck in a perpetual loop of wishing because that is the state of your reality.

This gets even trickier when dealing with emotions and feelings. Let's say you are jealous of someone else's success or accomplishments. By being jealous, you are telling the Universe you don't have those same abilities, talents, or potential. For instance, let's say you are jealous of someone who became an overnight sensation on some social media platform. Your jealousy tells the Universe that you have reason to be jealous. So, the Universe makes darn sure you don't ever become an overnight social media sensation so that your jealousy matches your perceived reality.

If, on the other hand, you feel happy for that person, believe that there is enough success for everyone and that you too can achieve the same in record time, the Universe hears your internal declaration and reflects that reality back to you.

These experiences of alternate realities, time-shifting, teleportation, and instant manifestation only convinced me that there was no limit to what energy, correctly directed, could do. It whetted my appetite and kept me hunting for more clues and revelations about the Universe. I naively thought this road would just get more wondrous and magical. Reality checks and dead ends would not come until much later.

Chapter 25

We Are Not Alone:
Angel On The Staircase

The journey into the "extraordinary" continued with experiences that made clear we are not "alone". I knew that entities such as the ghosts of passed-away relatives could appear. I was not aware that entities from other dimensions or realms could physically interact with us and even materialize items in our reality. This empowered me to believe that, with the right knowledge and tools, we could create or achieve anything in this life. This would prove to have limitations, with far-reaching consequences.

Angel On The Staircase

My dad was not religious. In fact, he often said, "Religion is a mental crutch." He was an accountant, and dependable things like numbers and logic were the only things he believed in. This all changed one night after he experienced something that defied both explanation or logic.

My parents' bedroom was on the second floor of their house. When you exited their bedroom, the guest bathroom was down the hall, on the left. If, instead of entering the guest bathroom, you turned to your right, you would be at the top of the staircase that led to the ground floor.

The staircase was L-shaped. There were five steps, then an octagonal-shaped landing, then the stairs took a ninety-degree turn, and eleven steps led to the first floor. This was not a carpeted staircase. The steps were made of a hard, granite-like substance.

Although there was a full bathroom in their master bedroom, my dad was trained to use that guest bathroom for everything except his morning shower. So, it was not unusual that night, when at 2:30 a.m., he ventured to the guest bathroom.

He was not fully awake, and when he reached the end of the hallway, instead of turning left, he turned right and took several steps, expecting to enter his bathroom. Instead, after a couple of steps, his foot met air instead of solid ground. It took him just seconds to realize his mistake.

He braced himself for the eventual and long tumble down the granite steps, thinking to himself, "I'm going to die." He then told me he felt someone holding him in their arms. He floated to the landing and was gently placed on his feet. When he felt the cold, solid surface under his feet, he jolted wide awake and just stood there wondering what the heck had just happened.

He looked up at the top of the staircase and realized there was no way his misstep could have landed him ten feet away on this landing. His body could still feel how the invisible arms carried him effortlessly to the staircase landing.

He decided right then and there that angels existed and never wavered from this belief the remainder of his life. When my dad shared this story with me, I believed him completely. My dad was not a frivolous sort. He was a man of very few words, and if he did speak, he was not inclined to tell stories that made him look crazy. I had heard of angels and family members who had passed on that made appearances and shared important messages. Never had I heard these beings could lift a 5'11", 200 lb. male like a feather. I realized there was so much I did not understand about the world.

Kevin And The Indians

One day, Kevin called me up to say he heard a weird message being whispered in his ear as he was waking up. He heard, "Largest gathering of Native Americans." This was not his thought, and he wondered if he was getting the message from someone or something else. He did a quick Internet search, using the phrase, "largest gathering of Native Americans."

What he discovered was an article mentioning pending litigation relating to the remains of more than three hundred Gabrielino-Tongva Indians (indigenous people of Los Angeles) near the Ballona Creek, close to Marina del Rey, California. The site was among the largest known Tongva cemeteries. But Playa Vista developers wanted the skeletal remains removed, as they were in the way of thousands of planned homes and condominiums in the area. Apparently, litigation was afoot, and the remains were dumped into storage bins near Ballona Creek.[25]

When Kevin learned of this, he wanted to drive out to the area, but he was unsure what he was supposed to do. He knew the message was not from his head, so he felt he was being asked to do something. He remembered I had recently taken a Theta Healing class, in which I was taught to help those who have passed over go to the light on the other side.

I was not particularly enthused to take this field trip. Marina del Rey was at least an hour away, and I wasn't sure what we were supposed to do. Because Sondra Ray lived in Marina del Rey, I suggested we visit her afterward.

We arrived in Marina del Rey and started driving around. It didn't take long to spot the huge metal bins. We drove around the area and stopped close by the dry creek bed. We parked and walked onto the creek bed. As we stood there, I stared at Kevin. This was his deal, so I expected him to take the lead.

He shrugged and looked back at me. "I don't know what we are supposed to do," he said self consciously. I felt annoyed and thought this was a ridiculous waste of time. As I was standing there, I started to see gossamer images forming, gradually increasing in detail. I saw a Native American male seated on a horse with a spear in his hand. Then more Native American males and females started appearing along the creek's edge. They were not moving. They stood silently, just staring at us.

Kevin noticed I was looking at something and asked, "What are you seeing?" When I told him, he said, "I think we are supposed to guide them to go to the light."

I felt a heavy sadness as I stared back at these beautiful people. I felt angry that their remains had been treated like garbage, with no respect. I said a silent prayer for them, apologizing on behalf of the land developers.

I did not have a chance to do the Theta Healing "go to the light" technique because as soon as I finished my prayer and apology, they started disappearing. In seconds, they were gone, and we were again alone on the dry creek bed.

Kevin smirked, saying, "See, I told you we were supposed to come." When we arrived at Sondra's unannounced, she had a guest for the weekend. He was a Native American healer who was doing numerology readings for clients at her condominium. Before we could even say hello, this guy says, "I am going to do a free numerology reading for you both."

We thought this must have been an unspoken thank you from the Gabrielino-Tongva tribe. The fact that there was an article that corroborated the message Kevin received convinced me that we are indeed not alone. There are energy beings existing on an energetic plane that coexist with our reality.

The Council Are Here: Help With Heartbreak

Although I have felt beings helping me with energy sessions, I don't share those stories here because I don't have any evidence that they aren't just figments of my imagination. When I say we are not alone, I really believe that. I want to share stories that, at least in my mind, show that there are energy beings, be it guardian angels, archangels, spirit guides, or even friends and family that have passed on. They are still with us if we are open to seeing and hearing them. I wanted to share stories that, in some small way, were confirmed by someone else present when it occurred.

During a rebirthing session, my client, a young woman, had just gone through a breakup of an 18-month relationship. She was heartbroken and inconsolable. I knew of nothing I could do or say to make her feel less despondent, so I suggested she do a rebirthing session to help with the stuck energy.

She lay on my massage table, doing the breathing. I sat next to the massage table in my usual seat when I saw in my mind's eye very tall beings standing around the table. When I asked who they were, they simply responded, "We are the Council."

I assumed they appeared in response to my pre-session prayer for help with this client. I felt for her and needed assistance. I watched them direct swirling energy to her heart chakra area (a spinning energy center near the heart). It was a lot of energy. Just as they were sending this energy, I noticed my client grimacing as if in pain.

I asked her, "Are you okay? What's wrong? You look like you are in pain." She said, "Yes, I am feeling pain in my heart like I am going to have a heart attack." I thought she might not panic as much if she knew the energy she was feeling was lending her healing, so I shared what I was seeing. She seemed to feel calmer after that. I told her to keep breathing, and we would discuss her experience after her session.

I witnessed more energy being funneled to her heart area, and just as I instructed this client to normalize her breathing, a signal that the session was ending soon, the Council stopped the energy flow and receded to the distance. They seemed very far away, but I could still see them in the distance.

When the client sat up to talk after her session, they were gone. My client reported after the session that she definitely felt less despondent about the breakup. She explained she still felt sad but that there was a peaceful feeling at the core of that sadness.

I would find out they not only helped us with healings but had messages if we were willing to listen.

Sacagawea Has Had Enough

I was taking a channeling class in Idyllwild that a friend was teaching. I went more to support my friend than any real interest in channeling; it kind of frightened me, to be honest. I believed these entities were taking our bodies and minds hostage and were force-feeding messages to us. I would find out in later years that channeling was just like getting a long-distance phone call from friends in different dimensions.

At one point during the class, my friend said she wanted us to practice receiving messages because, after the break, we would pair up with a partner and receive a message for them. She instructed us to breathe rhythmically in and out and relax. She told us to have a notebook and pen in hand to write down exactly what we heard, saw, felt, etc.

I heard a voice introducing herself as Sock-A-Ga-We-A. I did not know who this was, I am embarrassed to admit. History was not a strong subject for me.

I started writing down the message, believing it was intended for the partner I would pair up with after the break.

As I started writing down the message, I could feel the hairs on the back of my neck stand up. This message seemed awfully pertinent to me. Then she said, "This guy is not right for you, and you know it. And, all the TV watching and wine drinking are not going to change that fact."

I could feel my face turning bright red. I was dating someone that I knew wasn't right for me, but I was blocking the intuitive messages I was feeling inside. And, I was distracting myself from knowing this by watching television and drinking copious amounts of wine.

I was pissed. I felt like she tricked me so that she could slide in this message. When I told my friend my experience (I was too embarrassed to share it during the class), she laughed and laughed. She told me the identity of this messenger. She was Sacagawea, the only woman on the Lewis and Clark Expedition into the American West.

I found it interesting that there were beings intent on delivering messages to us when we were not acting in our best interests. I would find out later that my dad, now passed, would also help me when I needed him.

Thanks For My Glasses, Dad

I was in the Apple Store in the Glendale Galleria. I was looking at their computers and was wearing my prescription sunglasses. Because I didn't need sunglasses indoors, I took them off and laid them on the computer table next to me. It was crowded that day and, after playing with the computers for a bit, I left.

As I was heading to the parking lot, I realized I did not have my sunglasses. Panicked, I ran back to the Apple Store. No glasses. I hoped the salesperson who had assisted me had grabbed the glasses and put them in the lost and found. I quickly flagged him down and asked if he happened to see and pick up my sunglasses. He looked perplexed and said apologetically, "I'm sorry, no. But I'll check in the lost and found bin in the back room."

Because these were prescription glasses, I was sure they would be in the lost and found. My heart sank when I saw the sales guy approaching me empty-handed. He said, "Even though they were prescription glasses, I think they were taken anyway." He promised to be on the lookout for them. I left my phone number in case anyone dropped them off later.

I headed straight for the Galleria police office and checked if the glasses had been left in their lost and found. That officer took down my number and said he would call if glasses matching my description were dropped off.

I was so mad at myself. The glasses were an expensive purchase, and I bought them mostly to watch Tei's baseball games that were often played under bright sunlight. The progressive nature of the glasses allowed me to see far into the baseball field and also check my phone for emails and messages.

As soon as I arrived home, I opened all the doors on my Prius, and with a headlamp strapped around my head, proceeded to take everything out of the car and trunk. I wanted to make darn sure I didn't leave my glasses in the car and only *thought* I took them in the Apple store.

After combing every inch of the car interior and the trunk, I saw no trace of my sunglasses. I returned to the Galleria the next day and checked the lost and found at both the Apple Store and the police station, but no one had turned in my glasses to either location. When I returned home, I strapped the headlamp around my head, once again, and repeated a thorough search of the car's interior and trunk. Nothing.

A week later, I decided to let it go. I didn't really need prescription sunglasses anymore, and stressing about it was a waste of time. I was driving to pick my mom up from her senior housing facility for a doctor's appointment when on the radio, the Hawaiian version of *Somewhere Over The Rainbow,* by Israel (IZ) Kamakawiwo'ole, started playing.

This was an old song that didn't play anymore on the radio, and my dad's presence filled the car. *My dad used to play the ukulele, and this song was one he often sang.* I could feel his energy strongly in the car as tears streamed down my face. I silently told him how much I missed him. Then I felt something drop on my shin and hit the floor. I did not want it catching under my gas pedal, so I reached down, grabbed it, and tossed it in the passenger seat.

When I was parking at my mom's senior facility, I grabbed the object and took a closer look. It looked like my prescription glasses, but that was impossible. I put them on. They were prescription glasses. They were my prescription glasses. Without hesitation, I said, "Thank you, Dad!"

I did not know what this meant, but this experience was adding to my growing belief that we were not alone. Now physical objects could appear out of thin air. Interesting.

Chapter 26

Meeting Delores Cannon:
The Centre Begins

Before Kevin was forced to undergo heart valve replacement surgery, he desperately wanted me to heal his defective heart valve (due to a congenital condition, his tricuspid valve was a bicuspid valve). I worked on him for months and then years and could not shift his physical state. During this time, we discovered Delores Cannon. Delores specialized in past-life regression hypnosis, with a practice spanning over fifty years.

Delores started doing hypnosis for simple habits (i.e., smoking, overeating), but while regressing a client one day, she regressed that client to another life set in Chicago during the 1920s, in which she was a flapper. Her mannerisms and voice changed to such a degree that they fascinated Delores, who then began exploring this unfamiliar territory.

What resulted was a practice spanning many years and the publication of over 15 books. What interested me in arranging a session for Kevin was Delores' rumored success rate in achieving healings for clients.

She was so successful that her waitlist was a year and a half long. Supposedly, she would regress the client to a past life, where the condition originated, and after the session, the condition would resolve itself. For unknown reasons, re-experiencing or witnessing the circumstances surrounding that physical illness or disease in that life would result in the complete resolution of that illness or disease in this life.

For instance, if a woman was experiencing infertility in this life when regressed, she might discover a past life in which she died during childbirth. Taking that memory to the present, that soul may block any pregnancy, fearing the past will repeat itself.

Another benefit of her sessions was the guidance received regarding one's current and future situations. It was akin to getting a psychic reading. But, what was unusual about this guidance was it didn't come from her. She discovered many clients had an inner voice with great wisdom that she called the Subconscious. During a session, she would ask the Subconscious to provide guidance on life issues and situations. More often than not, the Subconscious would provide insights, accurate predictions, and helpful advice.

I was convinced if Kevin regressed to the life that related to his defective heart valve, he could heal without surgery. I called to make an appointment for Kevin and me and was told the next available appointments were 18 months away. I mentioned the gravity of Kevin's situation, and to my surprise, they scheduled us for the following month.

Delores' office was located in Arkansas, in a tiny town of about 1,900 called Huntsville. There were maybe two restaurants in the entire town. Her office sat between two businesses in a small strip mall (if you could call it that). It was actually a row of four businesses. The business to her left was boarded up and deserted. The business to the right was a hair salon and was closed that day.

She only did one hypnosis a day and said it could take up to five hours. We met her on a Saturday. The room looked like an industrial plant: large, empty, with a cement floor. The only furniture was a couch, a coffee table, and a chair for Delores. I suspected this woman, with her polyester jogging suit and white poodle permed hair, had a lot more going on than first appearances would indicate.

Delores sat us down. She said she would interview us to find out what we wanted from the session, then take whoever was going first to the backroom for the actual hypnosis. There would be an opportunity to talk again at the end of the session. We had not been talking long when there was a loud knocking on the wall close to the ceiling across the large room.

She smiled and said, "Oh, good. They are here." Kevin and I looked at each other then back at her. "Who is here?" we asked simultaneously. "The Council," she responded as if that would explain it. "Who is the Council?" I asked, now feeling nervous about this whole process. Was this a scam? Did she have people she worked with to create this knocking sound? The sound was very high on the wall, close to the ceiling, and the business adjacent was closed. If this was a hoax, it was a very elaborate one.

She said, "The Council helps me with these sessions." Later during the initial interview, I asked the Council,

"Am I supposed to take the hypnosis training from Delores?" Silence. She said, "Silence is usually a no." Well, if this was a scam, it wasn't a good one because she was not encouraging me to take her training.

We went to the backroom (I was going first). I was there to address the pain in my C4, C5, and C6 cervical vertebrae, in which I was told by an orthopedic surgeon had degeneration. The collapsed neck bones were impinging on the spinal nerves causing excruciating pain down my neck and left arm. Kevin had resolved the pain with Reiki, but Richard had warned me if I did not identify the core issue underlying the condition, it would return. Surgery was the next step if the pain returned. I was here to discover that underlying issue and prevent the neck pain from returning.

After laying me down and regressing me for several minutes, she directed me to see the life that related to my neck problems. I immediately saw in clear detail, I was standing on a wooden platform with a noose around my neck. She asked me if I knew why I was up there. I shook my head no. She directed me to regress further back so I could see the circumstances leading up to my being on that platform.

Then I saw myself in a stone castle. There were men in full metal armor walking around this castle. I was wearing a dress with a wide hoop with material that billowed around me. I was amused to look so feminine, as I am a bit of a tomboy. It looked like my husband was the king, and he felt very much like my present-day, soon-to-be ex-husband. He was talking to some men about details relating to an ongoing war with another kingdom.

Another man entered the castle, and I knew who that was immediately. It was Kevin. He was talking to my husband, the king. They were making some kind of arms deal. But as he was talking to my husband, he was eyeing me, flirting with his gaze. Then suddenly, I was in my bedroom, standing next to the bed. Kevin was in the room and suddenly impulsively kissed my lips. Right when this happened, a guard happened to be walking by the open door and saw that kiss. He yelled something, and several armored men barged into the room and dragged both of us out.

The next thing I knew, we were both on the platform with nooses around our necks. I died when the platform floor dropped beneath me, hearing the crowd yell, "Degenerate!" at me. *After the session, I found it interesting that my condition was called degeneration of the C4, C5, and C6 neck bones, the bones that would break if I were hung.*

After the regression portion, Delores called upon my Subconscious to give me guidance on whatever questions I may have. I remember asking if I was supposed to start a healing center. When I asked that question, there was vigorous knocking on the back wall of the room. Delores said, "The Council says yes, you are supposed to open a healing center."

I then asked my Subconscious where and how this would happen as I had been looking for an affordable space to rent for over five years. My Subconscious answered that when I returned home, I would immediately find a space to rent, that it would be affordable, and that I would get everything I wanted.

This transition would be so seamless that I would exclaim, "How can it be this easy?"

Following my session, we ate dinner at one of the two diners in town. This was a small, unassuming diner with booths and linoleum floors. I was exhausted and not paying much attention to my surroundings. Then when I had eaten a bit and felt more with it, I looked around the restaurant. "Kevin!" I exclaimed, "Look!" I pointed to the wall and the cashier area. On the wall was a crossbow and arrow, and next to the cashier was a fully armored guard statue, complete with a pointed spear. *Again, I can't make this stuff up.*

For those of you wondering what happened during Kevin's session, it was uneventful. He could not get out of his head and found the session unremarkable. But here is what I surmised from that. Kevin had a distrust toward allopathic medical doctors in general. I firmly believed that he was supposed to have allopathic medicine save his life, so there could be forgiveness and healing between them.

Chapter 27

Glimpse Of Level III

When I returned home, I was walking, down the hall, to my small, single-room office. The room was so small it barely fit my massage table. The maintenance guy was cleaning a large apartment. I asked what was going on? He said, "The previous tenants moved out." This, however, was a regular apartment, not a commercial space like the room I was renting down the hall. This was the only building in Pasadena that was a multi-purpose building, meaning it housed both residential and commercial businesses.

Downstairs were all retail businesses. There was a Starbucks, Dunkin' Donuts, and a metaphysical bookstore. Upstairs on one end of the building was a small insurance agency, a hair salon, and my small room to see clients. My room was so small that when moving around my massage table, I had to press my back against the wall and slide side to side.

Zoning notwithstanding, this newly available space was perfect for a center. It had one long rectangular bedroom but curiously had two entrances to it. If I put in a wall to divide it into two rooms, each would have its own entrance. The big living room would be perfect for classes. The kitchen, complete with a refrigerator and stove, was perfect for cooking and storing food for classes and other events, and having a bathroom right in the space was perfect for clients, practitioners, and visitors.

I asked the maintenance guy to ask the landlord if I could take over that space and if they could transfer my security deposit from my existing location to this new location. I also asked if they could install a wall with soundproofing to divide the long, large bedroom into two rooms and proposed a monthly rental rate. The maintenance guy told me the next day the landlord said yes to it all. He went on to say that building the wall to create two treatment rooms would be easy and that he had just acquired some soundproofing material from another building that he could put in the wall for privacy in each room.

I said, without thinking, "It can't be this easy." And, actually, it was, and it wasn't—like all things. I clearly explained to the landlord how I planned to use this space, and with that understanding, he prepared the lease agreement. In just a couple of days, I was in that apartment meeting with the landlord and maintenance guy to sign the agreement.

I read it, and my heart sank. The agreement was titled "Residential Agreement." I looked at the landlord and said, "Hey, this is a residential agreement. You know I want to use this space as a healing center." He shrugged as if to say, "It's not my problem." Then he said in a flat, emotionless tone, "This apartment is zoned residential. I cannot change that. If you want to use it as a center, you better change the zoning."

I knew it couldn't be this easy. What the heck do I do now? I told the landlord, "Okay, I will. I will change the zoning and sign this agreement later today." He glanced at the maintenance guy next to him, eyebrows raised. "OK," he said slowly. "Whatever, you say."

I did not feel as confident as I sounded. In fact, other than knowing where City Hall was located, I had no idea how zoning worked and how to change it. But, the space was too perfect, and I couldn't give up now. Twenty minutes later, I was at the Building and Safety Division department in Pasadena. There were eight windows with clerks helping customers. I scanned the room to see how this worked and saw there was a ticket dispenser. People were called according to their numbered tickets. I went to the number dispenser and pulled eight consecutive tickets.

This was my impromptu plan. When I was called to a window, I would find out what the procedure was to change zoning. I would fill out whatever form needed filling out, and then when one of the other numbers was called, I would be back, in no time, before one of the clerks.

When my first number was called, I explained to the clerk I wanted to change the zoning of my apartment from residential to commercial. He shook his head as if I was crazy and said, "You can't do that." I explained my building was a mixed-use building. He then said, "Oh yeah, I remember. That is the only mixed-use building in Pasadena."

"Okay. This is what you have to do. Because you will have more visitors than if you just lived in your unit, you would have to do a parking space survey," he said.

That didn't sound easy or cheap. "How do I do that?" I asked. He said, "You have to hire a surveyor, then have him survey the parking lot, then make recommendations for how many parking spaces you can have for your business. And, the likelihood of you succeeding after all that time and expense is not good."

I sighed and thanked him for his time. I sat back down in the waiting room to rethink my plan. Then suddenly, I had a wacky idea that I thought might just work. When my next number was called, it was for a different clerk. I took a deep breath and said, "Hi. I currently rent a commercial space in my building, and I am moving down the hall to another space." "Oh," he said. "Just down the hall? Would you like just to transfer your business to that other space?" "Yes, I would," I answered, smiling. "No problem." He prepared the forms, handed them to me, and directed me to register them across the street in the City Hall building. And, just like that, The Centre was born.

It took a month for the maintenance guy to build the wall and finish the other adjustments to the space to make it business-ready. It took another month to clean, paint, and decorate it. Just as my subconscious predicted, the business seemed to take off. I was interviewing practitioners and had some signed up to start renting the other treatment room for their practices. Instead of renting that room by the month, I rented it by the day so that more practitioners could use it. (I created what I wanted and couldn't find: A place where I could rent a room only when I needed it, instead of paying for a room 24/7, which I couldn't afford).

I had only been open for a month or so when my mom called to inform me, on his recent birthday, my dad had an aneurysm burst and was in the hospital. She assured me that he survived the aneurysm and was recovering. She was pretty shaken but hopeful he would be back at home in no time.

Two days later, my mom called back, but I could barely understand her. The sound I was hearing was of an animal in intense pain, yelping and screaming incoherently. The pain in her voice was unlike anything I had ever heard. I was in shock, waiting for her to tell me what I could not believe could be true. My dad had regurgitated three liters of bile while in a horizontal position, so he asphyxiated, then had a heart attack. The doctors put him in an induced coma and were hoping when they woke him, he would recover.

The Centre would have to be put on hold because I needed to get to San Francisco and help my mother through her worst nightmare. She and my dad had been married for 45 years and spent each and every day together. They were like peanut butter and jelly. She would be lost without him.

My brain was trying to take in this information. I had just visited him, with my children, the weekend before for his birthday. He looked much younger than his 75 years and appeared very healthy and happy. In fact, my children kept marveling at how young both their grandparents looked.

And here was the most shocking fact for me. When I visited them the weekend before, I worked on my dad, like I usually did, and I did the aneurysm code on him, which came up during his session. We had amazing success with that particular code. I had never had a client have an aneurysm burst. I kept wondering, how could this happen, why was this happening, why now?

During the week that my dad was in that coma, he deteriorated and became brain dead. The only thing keeping him alive was the breathing machine. My mother made the agonizing decision to take him off life support. I had never witnessed someone being taken off life support, let alone my dad. When they turned off the machine, he didn't stop breathing right away, which gave me hope he might miraculously wake up.

It took ten hours, and he did not pass until minutes after my mom and my aunt and uncle left the room to get food, as everyone was starving. I was told later that this was not uncommon. The living relatives are so attached that the person dying waits for them all to leave before passing.

It dawned on me that I had made assumptions that were unrealistic and just wrong. I had experienced so many healings (many might consider miracles) that I had assumed I had the tools which would prevent illness, disease, and death. This wasn't even accurate in my own practice because I had experienced failures before. But the mind is tricky. We can fool ourselves into thinking a lot of crazy things. I had thought all my healing tools enabled me to control and prevent death.

That belief allowed me to suppress any fears about life's unpredictability. I was face-to-face with the realization that we really don't know when or how we will pass from this world.

Part III

The Piece Within

Chapter 28

The Toothbrush Incident:
Or, Who Is Maile?

I was still getting my spiritual guidance at the Alexandria Bookstore in Pasadena. One day, I spotted a tall pile of used books on the counter near the cash register. Right away, my eyes were drawn to a CD set at the very bottom of the pile. It was called *Spontaneous Awakening* by Adyashanti. I had never come across any of his books, but for some reason, I had to have that CD set. I asked the cashier if I could buy it, and he said I had to wait until he input the entire pile into the system.

Forty-five minutes later, I was buying the set. It was worth the wait. The used price was much more affordable for me at that time. From the very first of the six CDs, this spiritual teacher spoke about Awareness and Awakening in simple but profound ways. There was something about his message that really spoke to me. *I still read every book he releases and have attended his retreats. He used to have a waitlist for his retreats because so many people became enlightened in his presence. Apparently, his CDs can have the same effect.*

A couple of weeks later, I was brushing my teeth when a strange thing happened. It only lasted a few seconds, but in those seconds, I would become so disoriented that it would take me years to integrate this experience. As I was brushing my teeth, suddenly, my consciousness (I don't know another way to describe it) broke off and was hovering above my head and to the left. I heard in my head the thought, "Who is Maile?"

It is so hard to explain in words what I experienced. After hearing those words, I saw myself not as a body with thoughts and emotions. I felt very detached from my body like I was looking at a character in a movie. Just seconds before, I felt completely merged with my body and mind. Those were me, and I was them. This felt different. Something else was observing that body and mind from a distance.

When I snapped back into my body, I was not the same. I can only describe it as my ambition button being turned off. I felt like the life I had been living and all the aspirations I had, were no more meaningful than real estate acquisitions in a game of Monopoly. I had no desire to accomplish anything, compete with anyone, or succeed. It all felt flat and meaningless. This feeling did not lift the next day. I felt scared and distraught about this new development. How would I make money and pay bills if I had no desire to do anything?

I am not saying this was logical, but I put Adyashanti's CD set in the closet. I think I blamed his CD set for this weird occurrence and did not like where it took me. I believed if I stopped listening to his CDs, I would shift back to the way I was before. This, it turned out, was fruitless. It took me six years to integrate this experience.

Chapter 29

If Life Is An Illusion, What's The Point?

After the toothbrush incident, I fell into a haze of apathy about life in general. I lost all enthusiasm for the activities and things that used to bring me happiness. I felt flat and lifeless, like I was mimicking my former, so-called normal self. There was no one with whom I could discuss this who truly understood how I felt. *Years later, while listening to an Adyashanti broadcast, callers to the program would describe this very state. These people no longer felt driven to set work goals and lost their enthusiasm for life. We all had the same thing in common. We no longer fit it into our old lives, but we weren't in that awakened state either.*

My ego, the shapeshifter, appropriated this state of mind and convinced me I was special (there it is again). I was special because I now saw life was an illusion, and this was a higher state of being. The problem was this didn't feel like a higher state of being. I felt like an empty shell of a person, with no energy and no joy.

Don't get me wrong. It wasn't as if nothing brought me joy. My children, their baseball games, their zest for life, and their playful nature brought joy. But there was always an energy of dissatisfaction buzzing in the background, engendering a feeling of melancholy and hopelessness.

It is amazing how one can function for years in this state, and no one would be able to tell. Then years later, in Adyashanti's new book, *The End Of Your World*, there was a chapter in it that discussed that people on the awakening journey may get caught in some common mind traps. He termed these as awakening cul-de-sacs, or points of fixation, in which some people can get stuck, sometimes for years.

He mentioned three in particular. The first one was a sense of superiority. Yeah, I can't relate to that one! The ego can believe that, because it has a taste of awakening, it is always right because the person has special knowledge lacking in others.

I could totally see I was doing that. I was wearing my discontent and apathy like an awareness badge, intentionally setting myself apart from the "muggles" that were satisfied running on their hamster wheels, which led nowhere. The joke was on me, though. My hamster wheel was worse because it wasn't even spinning. At least everyone else was accomplishing things.

The second cul-de-sac hit home even stronger. This, he termed, was getting stuck in a mental trap of meaninglessness. He said, "The ego's desire to find meaning in life is actually a substitute for the perception of being life itself. The search for meaning in life is a surrogate for the knowledge that we are Life."

In other words, the ego wants a job. It wants to be doing something. The spirit knows that there is nothing that needs to be done, and existing and being is enough. It's like your mother doesn't have to "do" anything to be recognized as your mother. Her designated role is cemented, regardless of her actions. You are an infinite being of light that has taken on a particular body in this lifetime. You are so much more than this body and its thoughts, actions, possessions, and accomplishments.

As a mental concept, I could understand we were infinite beings of light. As a practical experience, it was neither relatable nor comforting when dealing with the trials and tribulations of life.

Then, I experienced a different way of *being*. I was still on the hunt for the next healing modality to learn when I came across this book, *The Journey,*[26] by Brandon Bays. Brandon was diagnosed with a basketball-sized tumor in her uterus. She refused drugs and surgery and discovered a direct healing power from the soul, and six weeks later, she was tumor-free.

But, the healing feat was not what attracted me. Her book spoke of a side effect of that healing that was much more appealing at this stage in my life: a way to connect to your true self. She was talking about enlightenment without calling it enlightenment.

I discovered she had trained practitioners to take you on this "journey" and many reported they had, in fact, experienced what she was promising. My inner skeptic thought this was a scam of epic proportions, yet I promptly found a local practitioner and scheduled a session. The session was really expensive for me, $250.

I reasoned that they couldn't charge that much if nothing happened during the much-touted sessions.

The session took place at the practitioner's home in Simi Valley. She sat me in an armchair and told me to close my eyes and picture myself sitting before a campfire. She instructed me to invite people there and talk through past conflicts. I was surprised that the conversations did not seem to be coming from my head. I almost wished she had recorded the session so I could've listened to it later.

She verbally guided me through other experiences (none of which come to mind). They felt unremarkable. When the session was completed an hour later, I felt the same. No enlightenment rush, no feeling of bliss and enrapture. Duped, I thought to myself. As I left, I could barely hide my disappointment. But what did I expect, even for $250?

A month or so later, I received a call. That practitioner was following up and asking if I had noticed any changes in the last month. I was annoyed to be reminded of this bogus expenditure, but not enough to be rude. I told her I hadn't noticed anything different, thank you very much. Then she asked if I had noticed a lessening of mind chatter.

Then I realized—wait, I had. There were times when I found myself sitting in the living room, staring into space, mind completely blank. I would have to force myself to get up and get back to the task of living. I shared this. She laughed and said, "I think you have experienced a great change."

I remembered Adyashanti saying enlightenment was not what people expected. Many were disappointed by it, in fact. He explained that many people thought enlightenment was the perpetual experience of bliss. But this assumption was a mistaken belief. Bliss was a high experience on the spectrum of high and low emotion within the dual nature of our third-dimensional reality. In true Enlightenment, there was no duality of good and bad.

On the contrary, Enlightenment included both good and bad. It was the inclusion and merging of all energy. This inclusion of all had no emotional flavor. It was blank, empty, very undramatic. That is the subtle feeling I felt; not bliss, but nothingness. I was surprised at this rather unremarkable way of being. Actually, if I am being honest, it felt boring. I was still at a stage, and still am quite frankly, where the drama and the bliss still held a great attraction. I am told that when the drama gets to be too much, the subtle feeling of nothingness is more attractive.

I am embarrassed to report that I didn't remain in that subtle nothingness state. My mind, the great shapeshifter, shifted back on, enticing me with the next great adventure. For me, that adventure was the pursuit of the ultimate goal: starting my own healing center. I wanted a place all my own, to work among like-minded people, to help people out of chronic physical and emotional pain, and inspire them with new and unusual spiritual experiences.

Chapter 30

The 57 Versions of Chapter 17 or
The Three Levels of Being Revisited

You might be wondering at the title of this chapter. For months, I constantly wrote and rewrote this chapter, trying to simplify and explain a message that took me years to decipher. By the time my first book was almost done, I had 57 versions of what was going to be Chapter 17. At the eleventh hour, I could still not get the chapter to fit in that book's discussion. My friend Archna teased me, saying, "I think you should write a book and call it 'The Fifty-Seven Versions of Chapter 17'." So now you know the backstory of this chapter title.

Over the years, as life continued to deliver moments of elation, success, failure, tragedy, and heartbreak, I kept noticing that the Three Levels of Being model seemed to encompass all that I was experiencing. The levels seemed to make more sense as I spiritually matured. I also noticed that traveling through the levels was not linear. It was more of jumping around depending on the circumstances of your life type of a journey.

The Three-Level model became a type of koan (unsolvable paradox for the mind). I was collecting realizations as I learned more about energy over the years. For instance, our thoughts, feelings, and beliefs generate different voltages of energy and can materialize as physical matter. When we act in ways that contradict how we feel, this conflict of energy causes eventual bodily dysfunction, pain, and disease. If you generate enough sustained energy coupled with strong intent, healing, manifestation, and inspired creativity are possible. (This realization was especially fun because it fed my love of control).

Along with these energetic realizations, I realized that manifesting and healing at Level Two seemed to empower, but it required a lot of attention and energy, and the results were inconsistent. It dawned on me that manifesting and healing at Level II was linear. What I mean is the progression went in a straight line.

For healing, if you were working on a cyst, you put your fingers on the lump and directed energy to it until it slowly dissolved. The progression of dissolution was gradual. Healing from a quantum standpoint was instant and did not seem gradual. For instance, I once discovered a pea-sized cyst on my upper thigh when I was in bed. I felt too lazy to get up and retrieve my workbooks from my healing room, so I held the cyst between two fingers and asked God to remove it.

I was somewhat shocked when I suddenly couldn't feel the cyst between my fingers. I slid my fingers up and down and around my upper thigh, but I could not find the cyst. You would think this would amaze and delight me, but it had the opposite effect. I was dismayed that the process could have been done so fast without me. I began to believe that my practice was just a waste of time and an ego-feeding activity. I stopped practicing for two months until I received irrefutable confirmation from the Universe that I was supposed to continue healing for my learning and growth.

I want to make clear that by sharing this story, I by no means intend to imply that if you ask God to remove pain, illness, and disease, He or she will do so instantly. I strongly believe that random incidents, like this one, were teaching moments for me. When I experienced the grapefruit-sized cysts dissolving under my fingertips, this was not intended to put me in the large cyst removal business. It was intended to show me that energy directed with intent could effect physical change.

This experience started me thinking that perhaps empowerment and control were not the "pot of gold" of my dreams. Yes, it was possible to manifest things with the proper focus and concentrated effort. But, it also required constant and focused attention, directing energy to the desired goal or desire. It was also linear, which meant it took time for the energy to build toward that eventual reality. I noticed there was a faster, more immediate way to manifest that didn't require concentrated effort and attention. This type of manifestation was instant, effortless, but also out of my control. This difference in manifestation processes intrigued me.

For example, during my divorce, while waiting for my monetary share of the marital home, my realtor warned me not to wait but to look for a house right away. The divorce dragged on for three years, and during that entire time, I looked for a house I could afford. Every morning, for those three years, I would search the new listings at 3 a.m. and visit the listings I could afford. It got to the point that my realtor began referring to me as the third member of her team and would often call me for details about a new listing.

I felt discouraged because the real estate prices had quadrupled since we bought our first house in the early '90s. A 30-year mortgage on a house I didn't really want felt like a prison sentence. For that entire three-year period, every house I liked ended up in a bidding war that began where my finances ended.

When the funds finally came through three years later, I decided to give up. There was nothing wrong with renting. I would rather rent a space I liked than buy an overpriced space I hated. I remember the next moments like it was yesterday. I didn't know this at the time, but I did what is called the tantrum prayer—a prayer made in frustration and anger. Not to encourage anyone out there to yell at God, but I have heard these prayers can be effective.

I said, "God, if you want me to have a house, you find it. I am officially done." And I was. I let it go and went on with my life. What I did not know was throughout that three-year period, things were in the works which I knew nothing about. During two years of that three-year house search, an out-of-state builder was building three brand new houses on an empty lot, close to, but not in, the nearby valuable housing market. That distinction, "close to but not in", was a crucial mistake for the builder.

That location was in an area with a not-so-desirable school district that didn't command the same outrageous prices he had been banking on. He had built these houses, assuming that short distance made no difference. As the houses were being built, the builder had put For Sale signs up in front of them. But because these houses were on the end of a cul-de-sac, they didn't get a lot of through traffic.

Two doors down from those houses lived a good friend of my realtors' assistant. During an after-dinner stroll, she had seen the signs, wrote down the phone numbers, and called to find out more about the houses. She had heard nothing from the builders until the day after I said that tantrum prayer.

On that day, two of the houses were already sold without being listed. The builder, now realizing his mistake, was offloading the houses at a loss and was anxious to move on to his other building projects. Only one house was left, and it was still not listed.

This assistant called me, much like she had done many times over the past three years, urging me to meet at this address right away. I told her I was not interested and was done looking for a house. She practically begged me to meet her, saying that this house is everything you have been looking for and is within your price range.

She convinced me, and I rushed to meet her. Mind you, I met her just two days after my prayer. When I arrived, I was shocked to see this house had everything I had wanted but could not find in an affordable house. My realtor got involved now and advised me to make an offer lower than the asking price, so my loan would be approved.

I told her, "No, what if my price starts a bidding war and I lose it?" She urged me to make that offer and trust her. We made the offer, and the builder, contrary to all my experiences during that three-year housing hunt, accepted it without making a counteroffer. Three days after that prayer, I was in escrow on a brand-new house. When I visited the house a week later, there were twenty business cards on the kitchen counter from other realtors, but I was already in escrow. Because the house was never listed, no one knew about the house, except people that lived in that neighborhood, including my realtor's assistant.

Once in the house, I realized how expensive it was to furnish. I was visiting my daughter's room at her dad's house and asked him if I could take her bed frame to my house, as I had originally purchased and built that bed frame. The bed was no longer sold at IKEA, and I could not afford it now in any event. He said the bed frame stayed in her room. He didn't want anything changed.

Trying again for the Universe to make it happen, I said a prayer to help me find this bed frame. Then I let it go. A couple of days later, I was on my way to visit a friend. She had hurt her ankle and couldn't walk, and asked if there was something I could do to help her. (I don't know if helping others strengthens the energy of this prayer, but both times I experienced this phenomenon, I was on my way to help someone.)

I usually park in the back alley, but she said to come in the front door. As fate would have it, I forgot and parked in the back alley. Right behind her house were pieces of white wood stacked neatly against the wall. Because I had built that bed frame myself, I recognized the pieces immediately. This was the exact IKEA bed frame I wanted. Not only that, the person had put all the hardware and the building instructions in a large Ziploc bag and draped it over the headboard. I immediately loaded all the pieces in my van, shaking my head at this weird coincidence. My friend said she and her boyfriend had been thinking of taking the item but couldn't figure out what it was, so they left it in the alley.

Both these incidents happened quickly and effortlessly. For me, these events cemented my belief that results done quantumly without my intervention and control were achieved faster and with less effort and stress.

I knew that no matter how many tools and techniques I amassed in my energy toolbox, there was a limit to what I could control. I started taking a closer look at Level III: Surrender.

I was contemplating the Three Levels of Being model, and one day, I had an idea. What if I studied that model using energy instead of people? What if I thought of the three levels in terms of energy instead of behavior? When I looked up the different types of energy, the science was too complicated and hard to understand. Yet when I looked at the different forms of matter (solid, liquid, and gas) and their energetic qualities, everything fell into place. I will explain the three levels in more detail below, but for those readers that prefer the summary punchline, here it is:

Level I (solid) has energy that cannot change form, so you are a victim stuck in place;

Level II (liquid) has faster-moving molecules that can change form, but only in a linear fashion;

Level III (gas) has even faster-moving molecules and can move in any direction.

The Three Levels Of Being Revisited

"We are not human beings having a spiritual experience. We are spiritual beings having a human experience."
—*Pierre Teilhard De Chardin*

This discussion follows the progression of water from its solid form, ice, to its liquid form, water, to its gas form, air. When we are most identified with our bodies, we are farthest from our True Essence (our spirit form, or gas). The lighter our form identity, the closer we are to realizing our True Essence, hence En-Lightenment.

When we realize we are spirit, we are lighter, both figuratively and literally. Think of it this way. Remember the game Hotter, Colder? In this game, the group picks an object that the person who is "it" has to find. As the person wanders around the room, the group yells either, "You are getting warmer," or "You are getting colder," or "You are ice cold," or "You are red hot."

If our purpose here on Earth is to find our "True Self", then the Three Levels of Being indicates where we are on that journey. The following is my theory on how we progress through these levels toward our realization of our "True Selves".

Level I: Solid—Ice—Reaction—Victim

At Level I, we are the coldest and farthest from our True Self. Ice is a solid, defined by having slow-moving molecules closely packed together. It has the lowest level of energy, and in science, it is said that the molecules are "locked in place." When molecules are locked in place, change, as you can imagine, would be difficult, if not impossible. People at this level often complain of feeling stuck or stagnant.

At this level, people don't believe their thoughts have energy. People who don't believe their thoughts have energy will indiscriminately allow their minds to wander in any random direction 24/7. If, as scientists say, we have 85,000 thoughts a day, imagine the energy this person is generating as they allow their thoughts to multiply like popping corn, unheeded.

Think of your future as a baked good and your thoughts as ingredients. If you randomly threw in garlic (I am not good enough), onions (I am unlovable), and bitter melon (I am stupid), would it surprise you when your intended lemon bundt cake ended up tasting like a garlicky, bitter lump of dough, instead of a light lemony sugar cake?

In other words, if you think negative thoughts about yourself 24/7 and don't think you are contributing energetically to your experienced reality, this is a victim mentality. Not taking responsibility for the energy created by one's habitual thoughts is the equivalent of stepping into a mud puddle and blaming the person next to you for muddying your shoes.

This level is characterized by a victim mentality because from this person's perspective, life just happens to this person seemingly at random. This person has no perceived control or responsibility over any aspect of their life. People with this mental attitude complain a lot. In fact, they complain as if it's an Olympic sport. Everyone else is to blame for all the bad things.

Now before you think I haven't camped here on numerous occasions, think again. As I said, we don't travel through these levels in a linear fashion but jump around them depending on our life circumstances. I believe it is a journey that requires certain realizations that can only come from fully experiencing the energy of each level and organically attaining insights and realizations from those experiences.

It is only when one realizes the power of their thoughts that they are ready for Level II. Only then can real change begin.

Level II: Liquid—Water—Free Will—Empowerment

At Level II, we are getting warmer and closer to our True Selves. Liquid has faster-moving molecules, and unlike solids at Level I, liquid at Level II can change, move, and transform.

At this level, one discovers that thoughts and feelings have actual energy fields that act as building blocks toward a future reality. Empowered with this mental attitude, people at this level realize they can create health, wealth, and happiness if the right elements are present. Accordingly, this level is characterized by Free Will and Empowerment.

I could recount the details of complicated scientific experiments showing that directed mental intention can alter both live and inanimate objects, i.e., changing the direction in which fish swim,[27] influencing the growth rate of bacteria,[28] ice, cold, wet sheets, drying up from the mental intent of meditating monks in minutes,[29] or healing occurring locally from energy sent remotely.[30]

Let me be clear, this level is not a simplistic, "Think positive about what you want, and if it doesn't materialize immediately, you have flunked Materializing 101." There are many more energetic factors that affect this level. *I apologize for another shameless plug here, but I do discuss those factors in great detail in The Infinite Now.*

But let's assume you have mastered the art of manifesting with the strength of your thoughts. What possible downside could there be when you are creating your desired reality with your mind's power?

In a society that worships the mind, there is little awareness that there can be negative consequences when the mind is making your life decisions and controlling your life. When the mind is the master, its goal is the pursuit of happiness and avoidance of pain. More often than not, that happiness is dependent on the static existence of external circumstances (health, wealth, possessions, relationships, exalted fame, and reputation).

If you obtain that laundry list of things that you think make you happy, welcome to the real hell when you endure the stress, fear, and worry of trying to maintain those achievements and possessions. You can spend a lifetime chasing happiness through the attainment of things and attempting to preserve your mind and body, never realizing you are on a treadmill that goes nowhere.

As one spiritually matures, discontent descends, and the desire for inner peace starts to outweigh the compulsive attempts to stabilize external life circumstances that refuse to be controlled.

It is at this point, if one is lucky, that the pull of Level III starts to tug at your soul.

Level III: Gas (Mixture of evaporated water and air)—Trust—Surrender

At Level III, the liquid state of Level II reaches a boiling point and reorganizes as gas. Gas contains even faster-moving molecules that are able to move freely, not just in a linear direction but in all directions.

When water reaches the boiling point, it starts to evaporate and transform to steam, then air. The person's life at this level is literally heating up, either because of unexpected or tragic circumstances or because their energy field has expanded to the point where an internal shift is birthed within them.

With an expanded energy field, the person's perspective changes. This doesn't mean they are better. It means they see things differently. It's like a person's view from an airplane is different from their view from the ground: An expanded perspective has different priorities.

This level is characterized by qualities of trust and surrender. At this level, the person has let go of the figurative steering wheel and allows God's will to navigate the course of their lives. Rather than steering the course toward their own agendas, they respond to the direction instigated by Life itself. This means they are fully present, attentive to what Life is presenting.

Surrender does not mean one has relinquished all control or goals in their lives. It's not a directive to don pajamas, camp on the couch, and do nothing. This level is not so much resignation as a spiritual maturation. If you think of the competing energies of our ego and spirit, the cross provides a good analogy. The horizontal arm of the cross can represent the energy expended toward material and earthly desires. The vertical arm can represent our upward spiritual aspirations. I think of our work here on Earth as balancing Heaven and Earth, or both directions of the cross. Right at the intersection of the cross is where I believe the energies of Heaven and Earth are balanced.

To me, this means that we still have our life agendas and our preferences and desires. But if Life doesn't fulfill those agendas and desires, we don't persist in our endeavors but accept what is before us and move on. I think Caroline Myss said it best in one of her books, "Knock on the door, but if it doesn't open, don't knock it down."

The reason I think this level is characterized by trust is we must trust that no matter what happens in the world, "All is Well." This means there is a trust that there is a higher knowledge to which we are not privy, but we rely on it to take us "home," much like a hiker relies blindly on a sherpa to guide them up unfamiliar icy mountain terrain. There is a trust that God knows what your heart truly desires and plots the course of your life to fulfill it.

It is my belief that the goal of all souls throughout their Earth journey is the discovery of your True Self (your infinite spirit) versus your false self (finite body, thoughts, emotions, and actions). Each person's journey may look different, but the final destination is the same.

These realizations collectively caused me to also revisit the question posed years before by my therapist, "What if you were just an ordinary housewife?" After analyzing the energy qualities of the Three Levels of Being, it got me thinking about the real energetic cost of needing to be special.

Chapter 31

The Little Known Price
Of Extraordinary

Remember that question from the couples therapist, "What if you were just an ordinary housewife?" It had been many years since that pointed inquiry. After many years indulging the self that craved and wanted to be "special" and "extraordinary", I learned being special or extraordinary had energetic consequences about which I was unaware.

Being special and extraordinary meant having qualities distinct from everyone else. From an energetic standpoint, this entailed being separate and apart. To be extraordinary then required one to be disconnected from everyone and everything else.

I had a realization that if we were all connected (because we were all energy beings entangled within an infinite web of energy) when we distinguish ourselves by being "special" we are energetically cutting ourselves off from everyone and everything else. Here is the confusing part. We can't actually separate ourselves energetically. We "perceive" ourselves as separate. In other words, if we believe we are separate, we feel weaker, even if we are not. In this way, we create an illusory thought, believe it, and then suffer from it. It's as if we hold an umbrella over our heads and then complain that we can't feel the rain.

I came across the famous quote, "I'd rather be whole than good," by Carl Jung, who was best known as the student of renowned psychoanalyst Sigmund Freud. Jung hid his metaphysical theories to maintain academic credibility.[31] (Metaphysics is the branch of philosophy that examines the nature of reality, including the relationship between mind and matter.)

Buried in Jung's research was an analogy that the whole of our psyche (mental processes of thought, judgment, and emotion) was analogous to a spectrum of light running from the infrared to the ultraviolet.[32] He didn't stop there. He went on to theorize that on one end of that spectrum is the lighter frequency of spirit that transforms into matter on the other end.[33]

For those in the back row, this means that everything from thought to body is made of the same energy, which only differs in frequency along that spectrum. His quote that he'd rather be whole than good makes clear that when we cling to qualities because we think those qualities elevate our value, we are tragically mistaken.

Think of a play in which there are many characters. Buried within our psyche are every one of those characters. We want to be the wildly attractive leading character, but one character in a multi-character play is incomplete and boring.

I remember complaining to my friend Richard (the awakening practitioner) that my rebirthing clients seemed to contradict themselves. One minute they might be complaining about their unsupportive, unloving spouse. When I repeat what they have just said, they do a complete about-face and then claim, "No, my spouse is amazingly loving and supportive."

Richard explained everyone has different "characters" in their psyche. These characters have different personalities and behaviors. For instance, one character might be the pure, saintly one, and one may be the slutty, promiscuous one. One may be the generous, friendly one, and the other the selfish, miserly one. He said, "Depending on the circumstances in one's life, these different characters make appearances wanting to be heard." And these characters were unaware of each other.

So, going back to my experience with clients, the one character who feels unsupported and unloved may come to the forefront and complain. But, once I acknowledged that character and repeated their concerns, they felt heard and retreated back into that person's psyche. The one who feels loved and supported then came to the forefront and expressed itself.

I saw an article in the New York Times recently reporting more than 200,000 minors had been sexually abused by clergy members in the Roman Catholic Church in France since 1950.[34] I cannot help but wonder if the characters that needed sexual expression within these clergy members felt deeply suppressed, such that this unconscious behavior erupted. Richard had mentioned that when characters in one's psyche are suppressed, they will act out in unexpected ways to be heard.

From this information, I realized there was no single set of personality traits and behaviors. Rather, we have many, many characters within, none of which singularly define us. In that way, even our personalities are unlimited and infinite. Specific behaviors and personality traits are just variations of energy expression. One expression is just one of many possibilities that we, as energy beings, can express.

In that way, again, we are not the single expression of one personality trait or behavior. We are infinite energy beings that can and will express that energy as varying personality traits and behaviors. So when Jung said he'd rather be whole than good, I realized he meant if we rejected any of those characters in the psyche, we were incomplete as an energy being or spirit.

Similarly, when we try to be special, we are picking one aspect of our infinite nature and using it to define who we are. This limited expression cannot compare to the infinite ways our energy can express itself through us.

For example, if our infinite energy fields were akin to a piano, us trying to be unique and special would be us composing a single song and having it define us. That one song (or job, or body, or act, or accomplishment) cannot represent the infinite songs of which we as pianos are capable. We are so much more expansive and powerful. So, when we embrace our ordinariness, we are, in fact, acknowledging that we are a part of an infinite, expansive energy field that includes everything and nothing. In this way, our ordinariness is the key to our omnipotence.

Chapter 32

When You Least Expect It, Expect It

I don't know for sure, but I imagine one's journey to the Third Level of Being, surrender, is preceded by a series of what I call "reality checks." For me, reality checks are those unexpected life events that make it clear that control is a convenient illusion we cling to, so life doesn't appear so unpredictable and chaotic. We know from personal experience that life can change in an instant, but we just don't want to know it.

I realized that all my metaphysical explorations might have been my way of distracting myself from this very real truth. In truth, maybe we all fill our days with distractions that allow us to ignore this fact: We are not in control but merely along for the ride.

Reality Check # 1: Healer Down

After ten years, despite my teacher's strong declaration that we were not the ones actually doing the healing, I secretly believed I was at least facilitating and helping the healing process. When people didn't heal, I had some rationalization why the system didn't seem consistent.

There were plenty to choose from because, admittedly, energy healing is complex. (I discuss this in great detail in my book *The Infinite Now*.) But, I had amassed enough successes for my ego to create a new identity: "compassionate, powerful, healer."

I don't know why I thought I would not experience a physical challenge that would take me down. I had been living with 15 years of chronic shoulder pain that was resolved, without medication or surgery, with the QEST work. I think I truly believed that if anything else came up, QEST would handle it. I believed this even though I knew of QEST practitioners who were helped, but not completely healed, of their ailments and were physically suffering.

Then one day, I felt an ache in my neck that ran down my left arm. It started as an ache, and I did some QEST codes on myself, but it wasn't making the pain go away. This went on for a week until one morning when I got out of bed, the pain was so intense I would immediately need to lie back down. There was some nerve in my neck that was getting pinched when I stood up, and gravity pushed down on my spine.

This terrified me because the pain was so intense. I could not stand up for more than a few seconds before I had to lay horizontal. None of my mental techniques helped me to feel less terror at this pain that was not going away. And I worried that my practice, my sole source of income, was in jeopardy. Who wants an incapacitated healer?

I went to see an orthopedic surgeon who informed me the discs in between my C4, C5, and C6 vertebrae had degenerated and that he was going to inject me with a steroid shot to see if he could get the inflammation down. I asked why he didn't suggest surgery (I was in that much pain), and he said he wanted to take a more conservative approach. He explained that taking out the herniated disc material and fusing the neck bones was not a quick fix and could have complications, as the neck has a natural curve that balances the spinal curve in the back. *Today, I think the medical field has other alternatives, like injecting material to bolster the discs so the neck bones are not pressing on the neck nerves and causing pain.*

In *The Infinite Now*, I shared how a combination of Richard Skeie (awareness work), and Kevin Kidd (Reiki), and Delores Cannon (past-life regression), collectively had helped me resolve this neck pain. Despite getting that pain relief, I was worried the pain could return. Now I felt vulnerable and realized that no one, no matter how many times they have successfully helped others, can control all illness, pain, and disease.

The Universe is mysterious in ways that we cannot predict or control all the time. I am glad the neck pain has not returned, yet I am open to the possibility that it can return at any time and that I may or may not be able to resolve it.

This realization shifted my priorities. Instead of continuing my treasure hunt for the next magic bullet for my energy healing toolbox, it was time to realize what was driving me: fear. The hunt was driven by fear and that pesky need for control. Now that I realized control was really not possible, I wanted to figure out how not to live in so much fear.

Reality Check # 2: Bella

Before my dog Jake, I had another dog, also black, also a Shih-Tzu Terrier mix. Her name was Bella. What happened to Bella was so traumatic, I did not tell anyone about it. When clients came to see me that hadn't seen me in months, they thought Jake was Bella, but just older and more subdued.

Bella was a bundle of explosive joy who indiscriminately loved everyone. Even seconds after meeting you, she would plaster kisses all over your face and wiggle her tail so excitedly it would move her whole hind quarters back and forth. She had this annoying habit of lunging at me when we were sitting on the sofa and plunging her tongue deep up my nostrils. She was so joyful that her presence was a blessing to all that knew her.

Now, those of you who live in the canyon areas will judge me for this, but my backyard is surrounded by eight-foot-high cement walls, and on the other side of those walls, I am surrounded by houses. And behind those houses, there is another cement road before the mountains start. Being a consummate city girl, I believed all this was ample protection for Bella to use her dog door and go into the backyard to pee when I wasn't home.

Because I was always home with her and took her to work with me, she was not often home alone. One day I was meeting a friend for dinner at 5 p.m. I returned just an hour later at 6 p.m. I worried as I stepped through the front door and wasn't immediately attacked by the joyful ball of black fur. In fact, the house felt eerily quiet.

Fighting back panic, I began repeatedly calling out her name, "Bella! Bella! Bella! Bella!" I had a sinking feeling in my stomach. Where was she? I ran across the street, and my neighbor was in front of his house. I ran up to him and said, "I can't find Bella. Can you help me?" He ran with me back to my house.

When we couldn't find her in the house, we went to the backyard. I was heading to the upper terrace wall when my neighbor grabbed me, turned me around, and pressed me tight against his chest. We had not in all the years as neighbors so much as shaken hands, so this sudden physical contact surprised me. He said, "Don't look." Knowing she was probably dead, and that something so awful had happened to her I wasn't allowed to look, sent my body into shock.

I found out she was lying on her side, with a large gash on her abdomen. I was told it was probably a coyote. *I discovered later that coyotes can jump over high walls, even eight feet tall, and that in our neighborhood, dogs should never be allowed in the backyard without supervision. I felt tremendous guilt that Bella had met with such a violent end because of my ignorance. I learned my lesson, and now the dog door is closed for good, and I am with Jake whenever he goes to the backyard.*

I couldn't believe this lively being, so filled with joy and love, was gone so fast with no warning. She didn't have an illness or disease. She didn't run out into the street and get hit by a car. She was just gone in an hour, with no warning.

For some reason, this event destroyed my false assumption that I had more time or that I had any say or control in my life. I was forced to realize that we really don't have control or knowledge when our time comes to an end. How many times had I heard of people who died in unexpected accidents or collapsed from aneurysms (like my own dad)? And yet, I was still able to maintain this false belief that I had a certain guaranteed amount of time before dying.

This filled me with fear. I was not getting any younger and could have a stroke or heart attack without any warning. I started fearing being on the freeway. What if someone had a heart attack while driving and caused a multi-car pileup? I found it hard to relax and enjoy life.

After some months, I was numbed to the thought of my impending and unexpected death and went back to believing I had at least some time before I died.

Reality Check # 3: Mom's Worst Fear Comes True

You know that lazy Sunday when the laundry is done, there are no work deadlines to meet, and you reach for that magazine or book ready to sit down and enjoy a cup of coffee? I was literally in a half squat with my butt on its downward journey to the couch when my phone rang. I glanced at my phone, prepared to ignore the call when I noticed it was a San Francisco phone number that I did not recognize. I always answer those calls because my mom lived in San Francisco, and it could be an emergency.

It was my mother's neighbor who lived across the street. She had been my mom's neighbor for over twenty years, so she had my phone number. She said, "Maile, your mom is okay, but the ambulance just took her to the hospital. I don't know what is happening, but they took her to the emergency department at the California Pacific Medical Center."

I thanked her for calling me and quickly packed a few things, grabbed my dog Jake and started my drive to San Francisco. When I called the hospital, I was told she'd had a heart attack. The emergency department, thinking she was having a stroke, gave her stroke medication, which had the tragic and rare side effect of giving her a massive stroke.

Here is the thing that puzzled me and my mom, but mostly my mom (and she wasn't puzzled, enraged). My mom jogged every morning for 45 minutes without fail. She rarely consumed alcohol. She didn't smoke. She ate copious amounts of fruits and vegetables and did not indulge in desserts. *We never had dessert after dinner when I was growing up unless it was someone's birthday.* Most puzzling of all, she had just had one of those life screenings you get to let you know if your body is healthy or not, and she received a glowing report of excellent health. Why then did she have a heart attack? My mom was furious at this turn of events. Her friends that ate the fat gristle off steaks and thought leisurely golfing via a golf cart was ample exercise weren't having heart attacks. They all seemed in perfect health.

My mom thought this was unfair. Even with her now damaged mental facilities, she had enough cognizance to feel outraged at this injustice. And this was her absolute worst fear. Her mother had a massive stroke, after which she was never the same and steadily declined until her death a couple of years later.

My mom spent her whole life doing things to prevent any chance of a stroke. Yet here she was. This went on my list of proof that, despite our best efforts, we were not really in control of our lives.

Chapter 33

Clean-Up: You Found
Princess Where?

After my mom's stroke, she was no longer able to live on her own. During her rehabilitation, doctors, nurses, physical therapists, occupational therapists, speech therapists, and the neuropsychiatrist assigned to my mother's case would pull me aside and caution me not to have my mom live with me when she was discharged from the rehabilitation center. They all noticed behavioral tendencies that they knew from experience would not be healthy for me to live with full time.

I knew I should take their collective advice, but I still felt deeply conflicted and guilty about putting her in a senior assisted-living facility. This guilt would haunt me even after she was situated and surprisingly happy in her new surroundings. Living on her own had become difficult, and having the company of others, being served three meals a day in a beautiful dining room, and having her own private room was appreciated after struggling on her own for so long. This was a stressful time. I was helping my mom with her rehabilitation (she insisted I be by her side for five hours a day during four weeks of rehabilitation). I was also cleaning out her house, getting it ready for the eventual tenants.

Cleaning out a house she lived in for over 45 years was no small feat. Every cupboard, drawer, and closet were stuffed to full capacity. Because I had only four months on this first trip, I rented her house furnished, so I didn't have to move everything out.

Three years later, when the new tenants were moving in, they requested an unfurnished lease. This meant getting rid of every stick of furniture and completely cleaning out the space, including the downstairs attic.

For this extensive cleaning trip, I took my son along. I needed his strength and sales savvy. We needed every stick of furniture sold or donated in a four-day period. I was so glad for his help and company. I was touched when he spotted my dad's custom-made black cowboy hat on display in his closet and asked if he could have it. *He would wear it when he went line dancing and golfing with his friends, who would tease him mercilessly. Then he would announce proudly, this was my Papa's, and they would leave him alone.*

As I was cleaning one of the shelves in the basement, I found a small box with a picture of my childhood dog, Princess, on it. I realized this was Princess' ashes. I was on the phone with my friend Archna when I made this discovery.

Her response startled me, "You found your dog's ashes in the basement?" I said, "Um, yes. Is that bad?" "Yes! Really bad!" she shrieked for emphasis. She explained, "That is death energy. You never ever want that in your house." I took a breath and said, "Then my dad's ashes in my living room for the past three years, not a good idea?"

"Are you kidding me?" she said, laughing. She didn't want to freak me out, so she said, "It's fine. Just move him where he wants to go, as soon as you return home." "What's so bad about it?" I asked, not wanting to deal with another task on top of everything on my plate.

She explained that ashes represent death energy and trap the soul instead of setting it free. She told me the story of her dad's ashes. When he died, she and her mother were living in an apartment with a carport that had a storage cabinet. Her mother, not wanting the ashes in the apartment, put the ashes in the carport storage cabinet. For three or four months, his ashes sat in that cabinet.

One night, her mother had a dream. Her husband was very upset that his ashes were sitting in that cabinet. With arms waving for emphasis, he yelled at his wife, demanding that she send their son with his ashes to India "right away". She was so shaken by the dream, she bought a plane ticket for her son the very next day and sent him, ashes in hand, to India, per her husband's wishes.

I asked Archna how I would know where my dad wanted his ashes spread, as he never told me during his lifetime. Archna said, "As soon as you ask the person where they want their ashes spread, you will hear a response immediately." While still on the phone with her, I asked my dad silently, "Where do you want your ashes spread?" I heard his response in my head right away, "Hawaii," was his answer. This made sense.

He was born and raised in Hawaii. I asked, "Are you sure you don't mean Dunsmore Park?" (This was the park in my neighborhood). Silence.

By now, the pandemic was upon us, and travel was not easy. Vaccines were not required, but negative Covid 19 tests within 72 hours of your departing flight were. If I was really going to make this trip to Hawaii, I needed some confirmation that this was really where my dad wanted his ashes spread. The only person I knew who spoke to relatives that have passed on was a channeler that appeared at The Centre for an event almost ten years prior. Normally I felt skeptical about this sort of thing. The messages delivered were so general, like "Your mother loves you and says she is fine." But this woman was both specific and very accurate.

I remember she relayed messages from loved ones, describing in great detail events that occurred in the hospital in their last days. She described past conversations so spot-on, the event attendees were in shock. This was why she had a several-month waiting list for sessions.

I hadn't seen or spoken to her in years. I looked her up on Facebook and sent her a direct message. I mentioned my name and when we last worked together, and how I needed to spread my dad's ashes and wanted to make sure I was taking him where he wanted to go.

I was pleasantly surprised when she responded right away. She said, "Of course I remember you. She said she had a cancellation for the following morning, 7:30 a.m. PST and would be happy to do my reading then." I thanked her profusely. I had actually never had a reading from her.

The session was going to take place on Zoom, so I thought I didn't have to get dressed up since only my head would be showing. The next morning, I was looking in the mirror and brushing my teeth when I noticed I had a spot on my Hello Kitty pajama top. As I cleaned the spot with a wet paper towel, I wondered to myself, "Is this disrespectful to wear a dirty pajama top to meet my dad when I haven't seen him in ten years?"

When she appeared on my Zoom screen, I was surprised to see she hadn't aged at all since I last saw her. She was and is a beautiful woman on the inside and out. She smiled, and after friendly salutations and sharing pandemic stories, she explained that she goes in trance to receive the messages from the person. She cautioned that she doesn't always get the person that we want to talk to, but more often than not, that person appears.

When in trance, she said she usually quotes the person, saying, "Your dad says this or says that, and does that make sense?" The first thing he said was, "Hey, I dressed up for this meeting. Do you like what I am wearing?" She said, "He said that and laughed like he was teasing you. Does that make sense?" I was shocked. If I had doubts about this process before, I didn't anymore.

He then said, via this channeler, "I know we had a period of no connection. Let's just start here." I couldn't believe what I was hearing. There was no way she knew that before my dad passed, we had a period of no communication. He and I could not agree about some of my life choices, and because he could not control me, he distanced himself.

His last birthday was his 75th, and the weekend before his actual birthday, I visited him with his grandchildren. I decided that, despite hurt feelings, I needed to reconnect and risk being rejected once more. It was important to know that I did everything I could to heal our relationship before either one of us died.

I cannot tell you why we flew from Los Angeles for his birthday. We hadn't done that before, but the urge was strong. And even though we had a wonderful, healing visit, it was short-lived. The following Tuesday, an hour after I called him to wish him Happy Birthday on his actual birthday, he suffered an aneurysm and passed from complications after that, a week later.

Before we talked about his ashes, he said, "I know what you are going through with your mom. I don't blame you at all for her living circumstances. I would have done the same thing. You are doing a good job, and you are a good daughter."

I started to cry at that message. The whole reading was worth that message alone. I felt tremendous guilt putting my mother in an assisted living facility. Even though it was a beautiful facility, it wasn't the same as living with me. I felt a huge weight lifted hearing those words. There was no way this woman would know this as we hadn't spoken in ten years, and we did not discuss this during our preliminary discussion.

Then he advised me not to make it hard on myself thinking of where he needed to go. He said I was really doing it for me and that he did not care. I knew in my heart, Hawaii, and especially the local beach where he grew up, would be his choice. Even after death, he was still taking care of me. Then, just in case I still had a doubt whether this was him, he said, "I think it's cute that Tei is wearing my hat." Whoa.

Then the channeler asked, "Is there anyone you know who chants in the early morning with beads?" That was me. Recently, Archna had given me a set of mantras to chant in the early morning to lessen the negative effects on my astrological chart. I said, "Yes, that is me."

The channeler then said, "I don't usually relay this information because it cannot be corroborated, and I think that it is therefore not useful. However, because this is you, I think you might need this information." She continued, "The woman says she is Julian of Norwich, and she says she is with you when you chant. She is from the 1300s, I believe, and was a puritan type nun."

Weird, I thought. I didn't think she and I had anything in common and wasn't sure why she would be with me when I chanted. I stored that information in the back of my mind and didn't give it much thought after the channeling session. I did share it with my good friend, Soko. She and I had been friends since age eleven, and she was more like a sister to me.

I was talking to Soko one day and described how one of the messages of this book was going to be "All is Well". She said, "Wait, where have I read that phrase recently?" She went on to say she did an Internet search about Julian of Norwich and found an article about her. In the article, it said she was writing a book during a pandemic when much of Europe's population was being decimated by the bubonic plague.[35] Her prevailing message was, wait for it, "All Shall Be Well".

I mentioned this strange coincidence to Kevin, my good metaphysical friend and confidant. I asked what he thought it might mean, and he replied sarcastically, "It means you better figure out what you are supposed to learn from all this, or you will be writing that same damn book during a pandemic, thirteen hundred years from now." Yikes!

These experiences were solemn reminders, not only that life changes but also that this life is not the final destination. We change rooms, and from our new location, notice loved ones, as if in loving tribute, are wearing our hats.

Chapter 34

The Piece Within

About eight years into my practice, despite all the amazing healings and spiritual phenomena, I was surprised to be feeling kinda blah about it all. Dare I say I felt bored? I was surrounded by what some might call miraculous healings, and I had the audacity to feel bored. How was this possible? I thought this was probably due to my unfulfilled dream of having my own healing center.

Then, two years later, I founded my own healing place, The Centre. Talented energy healers, including chiropractors, acupuncturists, intuitive, massage therapists, and past-life regressionists, were renting the second and third treatment rooms. Now I was doing my dream job, helping clients heal and helping fellow practitioners fulfill their vocational dreams. I had a roof over my head, food to eat, and amazing children. But, I still felt an emptiness within, a feeling of blah, a yearning for something I could not identify. What was I missing?

I then remembered what Christina Thomas Fraser (my first rebirthing instructor) used to say, "The road to God is not a circus." She believed all the psychic phenomena, including healings, were really the last temptations before the real spiritual treasure was found. All this was cubic zirconia: It looked like the real diamond, all shiny and beautiful, but was not the real deal. If one were content (and a lot of people are), one could spend lifetimes collecting huge piles of cubic zirconia, believing that the next gem will bring that lasting happiness and peace.

In Michael Singer's book *The Untethered Soul,* I read that there was a reason people feel so happy when they get what they think they want. He said when we finally get our heart's desire, our mind shuts off for a bit and the energy of the infinite is able to flood our systems. He theorized that because this blissful feeling coincides with the moment, we get what we want, we believe getting what we want is the key to everlasting happiness and peace. But within a few days, sometimes minutes, the mind turns back on and the dissatisfaction creeps back in, and the hunt continues. This is not unlike the plight of the addict, chasing the new high.

Most people think that happiness means feeling happy all the time, being in a good mood. But that happiness is usually conditional. If we get what we want, and people act the way we think they should, we are happy. This is transitory. It cannot be sustained indefinitely because we don't always get what we want, and other people have free will.

Joy, however, is different. It is a causeless state that comes from a connection to our true "being" rather than from our effortful "doing." I noticed a trend as I worked with clients from all socioeconomic, ethnic, and gender backgrounds. When all was said and done, everyone wanted the same thing when pressed for an answer; they wanted to feel more peace of mind. They were tired of feeling stressed out, fearful, and sad all the time.

In a workshop I took, the instructor said something that really resonated. She was instructing us to make a list of what we wanted for a future mate, but instead of the usual laundry list of attributes (height, weight, hair and eye color, occupation, personality traits), she wanted us to list how we wanted to feel when around this mate (content, relaxed, safe, happy, serene, etc.).

It struck me that all those attributes were external (how they looked, what they did for a living, etc.), and she emphasized we put that list together because we think if we have a mate with those traits, we will feel happy. It dawned on me that, again, those things were external to us. Even the relationship itself was external. We believe if we have a relationship with a certain person, who acts a certain way and has a laundry list of traits, that we will feel happy, safe, content.

It was an interesting equation. If I have "this", then I will feel "that". And, if "this" changes or ends, there goes my happiness. And, because everything changes and ends, this seemed like a perfect recipe for a lifetime of suffering.

Does anything in this life bring happiness without cause? Was there something in the external world I could become or attain that could afford me everlasting happiness? After a lifetime of searching for things, I thought I wanted to have or to be, I can tell you from personal experience the answer is no. I believe that is the difference between happiness and joy. Happiness is fleeting and is caused by getting what we think we want. Joy is a causeless state that is naturally felt when we are connected to the infinite energy field.

I thought about how each and every breathwork client would feel this peaceful bliss at the end of their sessions. I suspected that because during their breath session, they were uniquely connected to the present moment because when you connect your inhale and exhale, without pause, the mind cannot function. (Christina demonstrated this during one workshop when she had us do the connected breathing and gave us oral mathematical equations to solve. Making her point, we found we could not complete them while breathing).

Rarely does one spend an entire hour without the mind spouting off thoughts, both good and bad, throughout your day. When you spend an hour connected to this infinite energy source, you get a taste of your true identity, peaceful bliss. And the really interesting thing for me is that peaceful bliss has no cause. I call it "causeless joy."

At the end of their breathwork sessions, clients want to sit up and start talking immediately. I invite them to stay lying down with their eyes closed and savor that peaceful feeling. (Interestingly enough, that energy permeates the room, and I can feel it too.) I tell them that feeling right there is giving them a glimpse of their True Self. When the mind is turned off for that long a period, your true self has a chance to slip in.

I discuss this in *The Infinite Now*. The present moment is really the portal to the infinite. The mind that delves in the past and the future runs on thoughts. The present moment connects you to your heart's energy or love. The past and future connect you to the mind or your fear energy.

When connected to this peaceful energy, you don't have to accomplish anything, you don't need to do anything, and you don't need to be a certain way or have a million followers on a social media platform. You feel peaceful because you are connected to your true self. What a concept.

The mind, however, thinks differently and, despite knowing this, I sometimes still slip back into thinking that what will make me good enough, spiritual enough, etc., is something in the external world.

I recall attending a Whole Life Expo to support a friend giving a talk. I told myself that I would go straight to her talk and then leave without looking at the books and other spiritual tools and goodies on display.

After her talk, I was almost out the door when out of the corner of my eye, I spotted a dazzling array of sacred geometric wands and necklaces. I had never seen such beautiful items. The woman manning that booth was astute and quickly spotted her next sale. She wandered up to me, holding up the necklace I was eyeing,

Then she said the magic words, "You know this necklace emits the energy of God Consciousness." Oh, no. She mentioned the energy spiral of the torus and how this necklace amplified that energy for the wearer of this priceless piece. Throwing caution and reason out the window, I plunked down my already overburdened credit card (I mean, there is no price on God Consciousness) and headed out the door with my high energy prize.

Once outside, as the sunlight reflected tiny sparks of colored light off the necklace, I remembered her admonition, "Once you leave this booth, this sale is final." I was definitely away from the booth. Right then, something occurred to me. That torus of energy she claimed emitted from this necklace was nothing compared to the energy naturally generated within our bodies.

Contained within our fifty trillion body cells were trillions of energy tori that could generate enough energy to run Chicago's electricity for two months. (I read that somewhere, and I remembered it as I stood there with increasing panic and horror). This necklace was the equivalent of a fancy flashlight, and I, the wearer, could emit the energy of the sun.

It was a very expensive lesson and one that I have never forgotten. *I know some readers out there are silently screaming, "How much exactly did you pay for that necklace? Just how expensive was the lesson? Okay, because I would probably be that reader, here goes: One thousand smackeroos. Happy? I am an idiot.*

I started to think about the safety we feel when we go to the movies. As we sit and watch the screen, we feel a multitude of emotions, yet we feel safe because we know when the movie ends, we will return home intact, despite all that occurred on the screen.

I realized this life is no different. We experience many delights and horrors, but when this movie is over, we too will discard our bodies and take our infinite spirit bodies to the next location.

My daughter Haley used to have a recurring dream when she was eight years old. She called it the *House of Illusions*. The dream would repeat itself, taking up where the last dream left off the night before. In the dream, she, her brother Tei, and I would be given obstacles to overcome.

In one segment of this ongoing dream, she, Tei, and I were standing on the shore. We were holding hands. She turned to us and instructed, "When the big wave comes, do not move or flinch. It is just an illusion." When she shared this dream, I thought it was profound and perfectly illustrated our task as Earth beings.

This life is a dream, and we are tasked with remembering it is not real. Yes, it feels real because we are wearing finite bodysuits with finite nerves and cells. But the inhabitant of that bodysuit is infinite and cannot be destroyed even when that bodysuit is injured or killed.

It finally dawned on me that if the point of this earth life was to discover our "True Selves", perhaps that feeling of discontent, that feeling of blah and apathy, was an internal guidance system, alerting us we hadn't reached our final goal. That internal alarm was not a bad thing, but our saving grace, much like our nervous system alerts us when our hands have landed upon a searing hot stove.

Our life mission, however, is not an easy one. We are a combination of finite (body, flesh, bones) and infinite (indestructible spirit). Thus, yes, life was an illusion, but unlike at the movies, we are equipped with 3D suits complete with nerve sensors that make this three-dimensional experience feel very real indeed. Inside the 3D bodysuit, however, is a secret portal that connects us to our infinite selves.

Yes, the mind can generate fear by feeding us negative thoughts about the past and future. But we also have access to the present moment (your personal portal), via the heart, to the infinite energy field (some call this the Zero Point Field).

You can instantly connect to the present moment via your senses. So seeing what is around you, hearing a dog barking in the distance, smelling food cooking or the ocean air, feeling the chair beneath your behind are all connectors. When you connect to that infinite energy field, you have access to your power source despite the chaos around you.

It's as if you are in the center of a tornado. People who have been in the center of a tornado describe it as very still, quiet, and safe. So think of the world and all its craziness, and try to stay connected to that still point within. When you do so, it's the difference between being a glass of water and the ocean. If you were a glass of water, and an upsetting thing happened (you got fired, someone made a rude comment, your spouse wants a divorce), that dropper full of ink would turn that glass instantly black. If you were the ocean, that dropper full of ink would dissipate instantly. You have access to so much more energy.

If the movie playing on Earth these days had a title, I think it would be, *The End Of Times*. We are bombarded with mass shootings, fires, tornados, hurricanes, floods, earthquakes, erupting volcanos, and, oh, a pandemic. How do we, as finite/infinite beings, handle the incredibly overwhelming events happening in the world? Do we unite our energies and overcome the "bad guys"? I believe it is not what we do but how we do it. If we forge ahead, connected to our minds, thinking about everything to fear from the past and the future, we are disconnected from our strongest energy source and are therefore lost.

I believe our only hope is to make sure our energy field is the highest, no matter what our game plan is. That means being connected to the strongest energy field on the planet; God, or whatever higher being in which you believe. I don't mean to be religious here. I am speaking energetically. God is an infinite energy source (just like each of you).

The easiest way, I know, to connect to a high energy field in my experience is three-fold:

1. Connect to the present moment;
2. Think of things for which you are grateful (gratitude is a high, high energy);
3. Trust.

When we connect to the present moment, add gratitude (the highest thought energy possible), and do them both with an attitude of acceptance (trust), we add to the big bowl of infinite energy, the best contributing energy ingredient we can be. If each of us just tended to our own energy field and left others to do the same, every one of us would be doing our part to make the world a better place.

Or consider this. Picture the infinite energy field as a huge web, with each of us an energy transmitter within that web. If any one of us were down (connected to our minds), that transmitter would not allow the full force of the field to function. If each of us just stayed connected or tried as best we could, we would be doing more for the state of the world than can be imagined. Every client I meet wants to make a huge difference in the world. What if just being you, without doubt and fear, was your greatest superpower and your greatest contribution to the world?

It's not always easy. I know there are times when I am feeling so overwhelmed that I don't have the wherewithal to do anything, let alone remember and perform those three steps. These are moments when I have been in intense physical and emotional pain. During those times, I suggest calling on that higher power for assistance.

In the '70s (I am really aging myself now), there was this cartoon with a turtle and a Mr. Wizard, who would grant the turtle's wish. Invariably, the turtle would find himself in circumstances in which he needed to be rescued. He would yell, "Help me, Mr. Wizard!" Then the turtle would enter a vortex and be whisked back to Mr. Wizard.

Those moments when I am feeling overwhelmed and need help, I surrender my problem or situation to a higher power to help me. I know it sounds too simple, but in my experience, it has helped immensely. It may not solve the problem, but I feel a peace within that helps me better deal with whatever circumstances I am facing.

So, what does this all mean? For me, this journey of needing to be extraordinary led me full circle back to the realization that being ordinary didn't mean inadequate or boring. On the contrary, being ordinary took on a new meaning that signified being connected, not separate, from my greatest power source.

When extraordinary, energetically speaking, I was separate. Because in order to be extraordinary, I had to stand apart from the crowd. In my separated state, I was the fanciest, expensive flashlight in the world (that could and would lose battery power). When energetically ordinary, I was reconnected, and I merged back with the infinite energy field. I was part of the dazzling, infinite brilliance of the sun.

I couldn't help but realize that the pursuit and validation of "self" in the external world is like a hamster wheel; that has us running as fast as we can toward a destination that ultimately takes us nowhere. Our "doing" is the finite and limited coal-coating plastered around the infinite diamond of our "being."

Like that coal-covered diamond, that heavy black coating (our bodies, our bad deeds, our bad thoughts, our failures, our negative emotions, and feelings) has absolutely no effect on the perfection of our infinite diamond beings.

Despite every reason we can conjure that we are just not good enough, our perfect, infinite being is waiting for us to stop torturing ourselves. Right now, right this second, we are that diamond perfection… which is hidden smack dab in the middle of our "ordinariness."

When we embrace our ordinariness, we embrace our connection to All That Is and take residence in that which unites and empowers us all. Having taken this journey with me, you now know for yourself the power within that can never be destroyed or taken away. When you discover this, you will regain your rightful state of inner peace: THE PIECE WITHIN.

Notes

1   Jay Keller, *The One Thing: The Surprisingly Simple Truth, Behind Extraordinary Results*. Hachette Publishing (2013).

2   With the Divine Blessings of his Great Gurus, Shree Sanjeev Anand is a Yagya, Pooja, and Tantra Vidhya expert with over 20 years of Spiritual Disciplines of Rare and Secret Sadhnas, Divine Poojas, and Yagyas. He is well versed and empowered to perform many secret Yayhas, and Poojas that are unknown to the world, and were hidden from knowledge for many centuries. For more information about Sanjeev Anand, and the services he offers, you can visit www.yagyabliss.com.

3   Pooja, is a prayer ritual performed in India, by several Pundits (Pundit is a Brahman who is one versed in the Sanskrit language, and in the science, laws, and religion of India), for the betterment of one's life. For more information or to join a monthly pooja, you can visit www.yagyabliss.com or email yagyabliss11@gmail.com.

4   My teacher is Judith Heath, who has taught and practiced QEST (Quantum Energetics Structured Therapy) for over thirty years. For more information,

schedule a session or take a training course go to www.quantumenergeticshealing.com.

5 "Monday Is For Suicide, But Sunday Is For Murder" *Morbidity And Mortality Weekly Report* https://www.acsh.org/news/2017/06/15/monday-suicide-sunday-murder-11433

6 Osho was a spiritual teacher who wrote many books on awareness and enlightenment.

7 Paramahansa Yogananda founded the Self-Realization Fellowship. He also wrote *Autobiography of a Yogi*, and Steve Jobs, founder of Apple, was so inspired by it that he bought the rights to it and made it available for free on Ibooks).

8 Elizabeth Kübler-Ross, M.D. *The Wheel of Life: A Memoir of Living and Dying.* Scribner, First Touchstone Edition (1998) p. 177.

9 Christina Thomas,. *Secrets: A Practical Guide to Undreamed of Possibilities* Chela Publications, (1989).

10 For more information about Elizabeth Terrel you can visit her at elizabethterrelcoaching.com.

11 Paul O'Brien. Divination: Sacred Tools for Reading the Mind of God. Visionary Networks Press. Kindle Edition

12 Patricia Evans. *The Verbally Abusive Relationship*: *How to recognize it and how to respond*, Adams Media. Kindle Edition.

13 Quantum Energetics Structured Therapy or QEST (pronounced "quest").

14 Paula Martin Burns was a co-teacher of QEST™ when I took the training, more than twenty years ago, and was the practitioner who worked with my classmate Mary's son, diagnosed with terminal cancer. You can contact her at paulaqe2@comcast.net to schedule consultations and or sessions.

15   Elizabeth Terrel is the woman I met in the YMCA class who introduced me to QEST. For more information about her or to schedule a session, you can visit her at www.elizabethterrelcoaching.com.

16   A SLAP tear is an injury to the labrum of the shoulder, which is the ring of cartilage that surrounds the socket of the shoulder joint. Injuries to the labrum can be caused by acute trauma or by repetitive shoulder motion, i.e., pitching.

17   To contact Richard Skeie you can email him at DreamCanyonHealing@gmail.com or visit him at www. DreamCanyonHealing.com. He currently hosts guided meditations in English with Portuguese translation every other Thursday. You can email a request to join.

18   https://www.learnreligions.com/navaratri-the-divine-nights-1770198

19   Dr Robert Jeffrey is an amazing practitioner with many years experience and many modalities in his toolbox. You can find out more about him or schedule a session by going to his website www.drrobertyjeffrey.com.

20   https://www.healingfrequenciesmusic.com/royal-rife/

21   Judith Heath has been teaching QEST for over thirty years. She does client sessions and conducts QEST training. For more information, go to www.quantumenergeticshealing. com.

22   Paula Martin Burns was the practitioner who worked on my classmate, Mary's son with terminal arm cancer. She conducts sessions and has taught QEST trainings. She was one of my teachers when I trained in QEST over twenty years ago. To contact Paula to book a session you can email her at paulaqe2@comcast.net.

23   https://www.learning-mind.com/the-flower-of-life-a-pattern-that-makes-up-everything-around-us/

24 Christina Thomas Fraser. *Secrets.* Chela Publications, (1989).

25 https://www.latimes.com/archives/la-xpm-2004-jun-20-op-gibson20-story.html This was not the exact article Kevin found. This was an earlier article. The article Kevin found related to litigation that followed after the remains were allegedly not disposed of in a proper manner.

26 Bays, Brandon. The Journey: A Road Map to the Soul . Atria Books. Kindle Edition.

27 Lynne McTaggart. *The Field: The Quest for the Secret Force of the Universe* (New York: Harper Paperbacks, 2008), pp. 128-129.

28 Lynne McTaggart.. *The Field: The Quest for the Secret Force of the Universe* (New York: Harper Paperbacks, 2008), pp. 185.; C.B. Nash. "Psychokinetic Control of Bacteria Growth," *Journal of the American Society for Psychical Research 51* (1982): 217-21.

29 Lynne McTaggart. *The Field: The Quest for the Secret Force of the Universe* (New York: Harper Paperbacks, 2008), pp. 128-129.

30 Lynne McTaggart. *The Intention Experiment: Using Your Thoughts To Change Your Life And The World* (New York: Atria Books, 2013), pp. 181-196.

31 Bernardo Kastrup. Decoding Jung's Metaphysics John Hunt Publishing. Kindle Edition (p. 83)..

32 Ibid.

33 Ibid.

34 https://www.nytimes.com/2021/10/05/world/europe/france-catholic-church-abuse.html

35 http://www.stpaulsbellingham.org/lindsay-rosshunt/all-shall-be-well-reflections-on-julian-of-norwich

Made in the USA
Las Vegas, NV
20 February 2022

44245627R00163